POCAHONTAS,

ALIAS MATOAKA,

AND HER DESCENDANTS

THROUGH HER MARRIAGE AT

Jamestown, Virginia, in April, 1614,

WITH

JOHN ROLFE, GENTLEMAN;

INCLUDING THE NAMES OF

ALFRIEND, ARCHER, BENTLEY, BERNARD, BLAND, BOLLING, BRANCH, CABELL, CATLETT, CARY, DANDRIDGE, DIXON, DOUGLAS, DUVAL, ELDRIDGE, ELLETT, FERGUSON, FIELD, FLEMING, GAY, GORDON, GRIFFIN, GRAYSON, HARRISON, HUBARD, LEWIS, LOGAN, MARKHAM, MEADE, McRAE, MURRAY, PAGE, POY- THRESS, RANDOLPH, ROBERTSON, SKIPWITH, STANARD, TAZEWELL, WALKE, WEST, WHIT- TLE, AND OTHERS.

WITH

Biographical Sketches

BY

WYNDHAM ROBERTSON,

AND

ILLUSTRATIVE HISTORICAL NOTES

BY

R. A. BROCK

929.2
Rob

Originally published: Richmond, Virginia, 1887
Reprinted: Southern Book Company
Baltimore, 1956
Reissued: Genealogical Publishing Co., Inc.
Baltimore, 1968, 1974, 1979, 1982, 1986, 1993
Library of Congress Catalogue Card Number 61-49177
International Standard Book Number 0-8063-0299-2
Made in the United States of America

PREFACE.

I offer to the narrow circle it may interest, as well as I have been able to restore it, the Tree of Pocahontas and Rolfe, as it has grown from them as its root to its seventh season (inclusive) of fruitage. I accompany it with illustrative sketches of some of its notable products, within my reach, in order to relieve the blankness of it, by revealing something of its inward succulence as well as its outward form. I have condensed them as much as in my view consisted with my object, knowing how insignificant the whole matter is amid the great surges of the world it is thrown upon. The notice of Pocahontas is exceptionally long for reasons apparent on the face of it, involving, as it does, incidentally, the vindication of Captain Smith against the unfriendly strictures of some modern critics, and which all lovers of justice will thank me for introducing. In a few other instances, where undue space may seem to have been accorded, candor, I hope, will set down my departure from brevity from larger opportunities of knowledge rather than to unworthier motives. To this consideration of relieving the book from unnecessary encumbrance I have, with few exceptions, omitted from the Register names barren of progeny, as also, of the almost numberless *"pieces justificatifs"* obtained by me in aid of my labors. On the other hand, I have to lament the want of the completeness I sought for it as a genealogy, baffled in part by ignorance of the sources to apply to, and in large part, also, by the indifference of many to the object in view. To these causes are owing the many bare and unsightly limbs it exhibits, that disappoint the eye by want of their proper foliage. I hope, however, that these very defects themselves will serve to stimulate many, who will regret to see them, to yet supply these waste places, in some future reprint, with their proper garniture. I submit it as it is, however, with all its defects, as yet the best I could make it, hoping that what I have gathered with much pains may be accepted as an offset for what I have been unable to reach. If, as I have tried to do, I have succeeded in laying a safe foundation whereon others may raise a more complete structure, I shall be content.

I wish to acknowledge, exceptionally, the courtesy of R. A. Brock, Esq., who has supervised the printing of the book, making additions to the text, and who kindly placed at my disposal the illustrated "Bolling Memoirs," as published and annotated by the late Thomas H. Wynne, and which constitutes the basis of this Register; as, also, to Mr. Alexander Brown, to whose active assistance I am much indebted.

The Frontispiece is from a photograph taken recently in England from the original portrait of Pocahontas (London, 1616), yielded to my request by its present possessor, Mr. Elwyn, one of the family of Rolfe, now, and from time immemorial, residents of Norfolk County, England.

The work was executed by one of England's best photographers, and under the personal supervision of Mrs. Herbert Jones—author of "Sandringham," a charming memoir of the many Norfolk families, containing a most graceful and graphic description of the original picture—to whose kind and judicious co-operation in forwarding my views, I wish to express here my warmest acknowledgments.

The "Pocahontas" found in many "Indian" publications, and a few in oil, while authentic, are from De Passe's almost contemporaneous engraving from the original and the only one known. Except such, all so-called portraits of her are mere fancies of the artists. The Engraving necessarily inexact, and the copies more so, the only accurate as well as authentic reproduction of that painting ever published in the United States is that of the Frontispiece of this book. The Sun's work can never be false, man's never true.

ABBREVIATIONS USED IN THE GENEALOGY

b.—born.   d.—died.   m.—married.
M. H. B.—Member of the House of Burgesses.
M. H. D.—Member House of Delegates.
M. Va. Sen.—Member Virginia Senate.
M. C.—Member of Congress
M. U. S. S.—Member United States Senate.
J. P.—Justice of Peace.

LETTER FROM REV. PHILIP SLAUGHTER, D. D.

Historiographer of the Protestant Episcopal Diocese of Virginia

I gladly avail myself of the liberty accorded me by the venerable writer to adorn my little book with the following letter:

CEDAR MOUNTAIN, *November 13, 1886.*

Hon. WYNDHAM ROBERTSON, *The Meadows:*

MY DEAR SIR: I am glad that you have undertaken to delineate the "peerless Pocahontas" according to the truth of history, since after your right hand shall have lost its cunning, no one will be left so competent, from a thorough acquaintance with the history of Virginia in general, and a special study of this particular subject, to do the work, and whose blood relation to her must naturally qualify them to do it *con amore.* She deserves commemoration, not only for intrinsic worth and her public services, but also because from her have sprung so many of our best people.

I have read your manuscript with much interest, and consider it a valuable contribution to our historical literature. I congratulate you upon having procured from England authentic copies of the only original portrait of her, so that we may see her as she appeared to the eyes of the artist instead of through the medium of the engraved caricatures. The personal notices are of special value and interest. That of the unique John Randolph, of Roanoke, seems to me rather severe, and might be tempered with some lighter shades. I have one of the last (perhaps the very last) letters written by him. It is dated about ten days before his death to his goddaughter, Rebecca Matoaca Robinson. With much that is otherwise, it has gleams of tenderness in it that, to me, are very touching, like the plaintive bleatings of the stricken deer. It gives in sharp contrast the two chief elements of his composite character. The best explanation and apology for

him is that his mind often lost its balance. One of the most
exquisite reminiscences of my life is having heard his great
speech in the Convention of 1829-30. I was so fascinated that
I was unconscious of the lapse of time—hours dwindling into
moments. I have often been reminded of one of his pithy
sayings in favor of free-hold suffrage—viz: "Mr. President,
when we leave the land we shall be at sea."

I would suggest for your consideration if it would not be
well to give a brief history of the portraits of Pocahontas.
Your criticism of the hypocritics of our early history is
timely, as it may tend to elicit the truth.

The New York *Post* had lately a long article on "Arber's
Edition" of Smith's Works, well worth reading for the opinion of the reviewers as well as that of Arber, the publisher.

One of the most accurate and learned books on Colonial
Virginia is "Anderson's History of the British Colonial
Church." In commenting on the criticism of our Virginia
Burke, who said: "Smith's work is a sort of epic history or
romance in which the author recounts, like Ossian, his achievements in like spirit in which he fought." Anderson
says: "The greater part of Smith's History is made up of the
narratives of his companions, expressed sometimes in grand-
iloquent terms, but Smith's own language is remarkable for
its simplicity."

I wish you could have included Randolph Fairfax in your
personal notices, as he was (considering the brevity of his
career), morally and physically, one of the most beautiful
branches of this remarkable family tree. But, as you must
draw the line somewhere, and you have drawn it at the seventh generation, he is necessarily excluded, and it might seem
invidious to some to make him an exception to your general
rule. I don't know enough of the subject to revise your genealogical details. My own experience teaches me, however
perfect your copy may be, it is impossible for a family to
pass through that most formidable of steam-engines, the
printing press, without the loss of some member or suffering
such dislocations that its own father cannot recognize it. I
may venture, however, to say that Colonel Meade had no
issue by his first wife, Elizabeth Randolph, of Curle's. Bish-

op Meade's mother's maiden name was Grymes, and she was the widow of William Randolph. Bishop Meade had no Randolph blood in him, although the types make me say so in "Bristol Parish," in spite of my protestations. Wilson Miles Cary, the highest authority on the Randolph family, says that the wife of Anthony Walke was *Jane,* not *Anne,* as it is generally rendered.

This subject has the more interest for me because from her have sprung leading members of the church in every generation, and her blood runs in the veins of many of our clergy and laity, of whom I may signalize the Rev. Henry Page, missionary to Japan, and the present bishop of Virginia, the Rt. Rev. Francis M. Whittle, D. D.

Hoping soon to see your book in print, and with best wishes for your weal, here and hereafter.

Faithfully yours,

P. SLAUGHTER.

TABLE OF CONTENTS.

Pocahontas and Her Descendants.

POCAHONTAS, daughter of the Indian chief, Powhatan, the mighty Werowance, who ruled over Attanoughkomouck *als.* Virginia, born about 1595, died 1616, married John Rolfe (*b.*——, *d.* 1622, first Secretary and Recorder-General of Virginia and member of the Council) about the first of April, 1614, and left issue one child only, a son.

POCAHONTAS, as her name is in history, and as she was known to the colonists; Matoaks, reported to have been her family name, or Rebecca, as she was christened, was born about 1595, married in 1614, and died at Gravesend, in England, in 1617. History does not offer, nor has fiction ever depicted a lovelier character. She was her father's "dearest daughter," the idol of her tribe, the admiration of the English, and the very pet, as it were, of Nature herself. Her father was Powhatan, the great Werowance and ruler of all the Indian tribes which, at the advent of the English, inhabited Virginia from the seaboard to the falls of its rivers. He is described as a savage of a grave and majestical presence; cruel, yet not pitiless; stern, yet affectionate; despotic, yet beloved; brave, but wary and subtle, and not destitute of magnanimity. From him Pocahontas seems to have derived all his higher and better attributes without the harsher and less ingenuous ones. Thus esteemed by her own people, with whom she lived to womanhood, as the flower of her tribe, and entitled by the English "The Nonpareilla of Virginia," she passed and repassed, on errands of love and bounty, between Jamestown (as long as Smith remained there) and her woodland home, as free thoughted and unblamed as Una herself; nor, through her years of captivity and married life among the colonists, nor yet while sojourning among the blandishments and seductions of the Court of London, was a breath of scandal ever known to touch her name. We see her, in history, but by glimpses indeed, but these are all luminous with moral beauty, and verify one another by a perfect harmony of tint.

We first see her, a child of eleven or twelve years, interposing herself between Smith and the uplifted club of the executioner, and saving him from the death to which the politic foresight of Powhatan had doomed him, braving at once and prevailing over her father's anger, and leaving us in doubt whether most to extol her compassionating tenderness or his generosity.

After her first introduction to us at Werowoçomico, we next see her, a guileless child, naked, according to the custom of her tribe, attended by her "wild train," playing and romping at times in the streets of Jamestown with the children of the colonists; a spectacle as blameless as amiable, in the light of a true and broad humanity, yet not wholly escaping censure (as where-ever was there purity that did?) from some of the "nice sort," who would apply to it the conventional rules of artificial society, to which it is not amenable, and who themselves alone furnish the indelicacy that scandalizes them.

Next she is seen as a sort of ambassadress sent from her father to beg for peace and the restoration of certain captive Indians, which were both accorded, and mainly, it would seem, in recognition of some personal but unexplained claim of the artless intercessor.

"Jamestown, as freely frequenting as her father's habitation," she next appears coming to every few days, seemingly with the permission of Powhatan, on errands of mercy, "bringing with her swarthy retinue so much provision to feed us that else we had directly starved"; and still, "during the time of two or three years, was the instrument, under God, to preserve this colonie from death, famine, and other confusion, which, if, in those times, it had been once dissolved, Virginia might have line [lain,] as it was at our first arrivall, to this day."

When, after Smith's return to England, the Indians "did spoile and murther all they encountered," we find that, out of a band of thirty, all were slain save one that escaped, and one, a boy, Henry Spelman, "that Pocahontas saved, and who by

her means lived many yeres amongst the Potawomekes,"
serving often afterwards as an interpreter between the colonists and the Indians.

We next see her coming through the "dark and irksome"
night to warn Smith against a planned surprise, and with
watery eyes, begging him to escape her father's fury; whereby the colony was, it is probable, a second time saved from
destruction. What but the love and admiration Smith first
inspired her with, and the natural impulse to protect again
the life she had already once saved, can sufficiently account
for, as this conjecture does, this new intervention?

As if her mission were to be ever in place to watch over the
safety of this young exposed germ of a future empire, she is
now seen hiding from his pursuers, Richard Wyffin, a messenger to Smith (who was then at Pamaunkee) whereby he was
enabled to timely advertise the latter of a new attempt on his
life, projected by Powhatan, which Smith, thus forewarned,
took good means to frustrate.

We now lose any clear sight of her for two years, but she
had evidently fled away from the beginning scenes of vio-
lence and blood immediately ensuing on Smith's departure
from Virginia, to live with the Potawomekes, where, her
retreat at last being discovered, one wilier savage than those
she dealt with, Argall, prevailed over the cupidity of their
simple-minded king to betray her, "reluctant" (as he states)
"into his hands" [April, 1613].*

In honored captivity she now lived a year in the charge
of Sir Thomas Dale and the Rev. Alexander Whitaker, than
whom two higher or purer men never came to Virginia. Being by them carefully instructed and fashioned to piety and
civility, a docile pupil, she now confessed faith of Jesus Christ
("which thing Sir Thomas Dale had labored a long time to
ground in her"), was baptized, and became the wife of "John
Rolfe, (April, 1614,) an English gentleman," highly esteemed,—adopting his religion, his civilization, and his language.
Her marriage had the sanction of her father. It was held
mutually as a new pledge of the pacification recently before
made between Dale and Powhatan, and which it is apparent,

---

*"Exceeding pensive and discontented, yet extraordinary courteous
usage, by little and little, at length wrought her to patience, and so to
Jamestown she was brought."

her captivity with the English and expressed regard for them, alone rendered possible. It at once allayed distrust, restored intercourse, and revived good-will, so that in Hamor's quaint language, "the colony was never better." Indeed, as more than once before, her intervention had saved the young settlement from destruction, so now, from her marriage to her death, she may be said to have hovered over it as a brooding dove of peace.

Finally, at London, we find her provided for as the guest of the Virginia Company, the honored recipient of the marked notice and attention of the Queen and ladies of the Court, and entertained with special and extraordinary "state, festival, and pomp" by the Lord Bishop of London (as described by Purchas, who was present), closing, untimely, her pure and beautiful life at Gravesend when about to embark for Virginia, [in a vessel of the Virginia Company specially furnished for her accommodation].

In one of its Registers at this day is still found this brief record:

"1616—March 21. Rebecca Wrolfe, wyffe of Thomas Wrolfe, gent. A Virginia lady borne, was buried in the chauncel."

These incidents of her life reveal a character of rare beauty and worth. There is nothing of myth or legend, of the miraculous or incredible about them, save to disbelievers in the higher virtues of human nature. Except such of them as could be known to Smith only, they rest on various and unimpugned authorities. On the faith of them, the Queen and Court of England, its highest and best people, and, in an especial manner, the Bishop of London, bestowed on her marked and distinguished attentions, inconceivable to have been extended to her, except as the meed of extraordinary virtues, and that in the presence and midst of many, who, had the testimonies to them been capable of being disproved, could have readily furnished the means, as some of them were known not to be wanting in the will, to disprove them. And on the like faith in them, History, and Poetry, and Art, have vied with one another in their several ways, in investing her name, from that day to the present, with a halo of surpassing brightness.

Now, at the end of two centuries and a half, the best known and most dazzling, but hardly most honoring of these incidents—Smith's rescue before Powhatan—is impeached by some modern critics as fabulous—most notably by Charles Deane, LL.D., to whose careful and usually candid labors we owe so much, and, in a very different spirit, by the Rev. E. D. Neill, D. D. The latter writer, indeed, seems to have exhausted, in his chapter entitled "Pocahontas and her Companions," all the arts of the *suggestio* and the *suppressio*, of innuendo and perversion, not only to throw doubts on much of her hitherto all accepted history, but even to blur her good name; nor, seemingly, without effect, for a gentleman, whose long avowed dedication of his pen to the sole service of what he esteems to be truth would give almost irresistible weight to his conclusions, when unwarped by prejudice or unbetrayed by false guides (Mr. Dawson, of New York), has allowed himself to accept, and proclaim as true, all adverse criticism anywhere arrived at, or surmised, both in regard to Pocahontas and to Smith. He sums it all up in a few words, yet so concise and comprehensive, that I cite them for such comment as they seem to call for, and the scope of this little work restricts me to. A proper reply to the more elaborate misstatements of Dr. Neill, has been ably made by W. Wirt Henry, Esq.

In some strictures he makes on Mr. Stephens's History of the United States, Mr. Dawson arraigns that gentleman for "repeating the exploded story of Pocahontas rescuing Captain Smith"; and "the old story of her alliance with Rolfe; her voyage to England and death there, repeated in the same old form; and in utter defiance of the undoubted fact of her early lasciviousness, of her marriage to an Indian, her subsequent adultery with John Rolfe, who was another woman's husband, and her ultimate death while the wife, so-called, of one Thomas Wrothe; both her so-called former husbands being yet living." [Hist. Magazine, N. Y., Sept., 1873.]

This is surely the most amazing mixture of ignorance and misrepresentation ever seen in print—wholly unaccountable for except on one of the hypotheses I have before suggested. Let us consider it. I will suppose that, at least, "the old story in the old form" of the voyage and death of Pocahontas, are not among the matters meant to be included in the sweeping "defiance" of the facts concerning her imputed to Mr. Stephens by this writer. The other points of the indictment (only remarking that I write remote from libraries, and from

an imperfect armory of authorities, but furnishing all that I
believe necessary to eludicate these questions) I proceed to
notice, in turn, as presented:

"The exploded Story of Pocahontas rescuing Captain Smith."

Necessarily the story of the rescue must have come originally from Smith. All the first published narratives of it
are his, or fairly referable to him. These publications are, in
the order of dates, His Letter to the Queen, 1616; his General
History, 1624; Purchas's Pilgrimage, 1626; and his "New
England Trials, 1624," where it is referred to.

Its absence from the "True Relation," 1618, he may or may
not be responsible for. That was neither published nor supervised by him. There are points connected with it never yet,
nor probably ever, now, to be cleared up. Its first copies have
as many as three different fathers, all spurious or anony-
mous, and the true publisher still remains unknown. That the
body of the book was Smith's there can be no doubt, but just
as little that no single passage can be asserted positively to be
as he wrote it. It is apparent that it was published for a purpose, and it is avowed that parts of the original MS. were
suppressed.

What was never in it, or what being in, this unknown editor esteemed, as he has it, "fit to be private and suppressed,"
none can ever know. Holding it quite unimportant either
way, my conjecture is, that the story was contained in it and
suppressed. By comparing the two accounts of Smith's re-
ception by Powhatan—"True Relation" and Smith's General
History—it is seen, as it strikes me, that the sudden and awk-
ward transition from the description of the scene in the former, "their heads painted in redde, and with such a grave and
majestical countenance, etc; he kindly welcomed me, etc.,"
needs bridging over, and that this need between a similar
point in the description and Powhatan's welcoming him as a
friend, after two days' of suspense and terrorizing in the latter, is naturally supplied, and consisted, probably, of this
very story of the rescue. My conclusion, therefore is, that
this story was *in* the MS., and of the matters the editor
thought fit to suppress; but, though not printed, was nevertheless known, so that no surprise seems to have been occasioned by its appearance in the letter to the Queen.

But in the dark as we are as to what was left out, or may
have been put into, that publication, only with certainty that
it was not an accurate reproduction of Smith's original, it is
alike illogical and unjust to hold Smith responsible for the
presence or absence, in it or from it, of any specific passage
or fact inconsistent with his own avowed statements.

The intimation, which has been thrown out that Smith
gave the preference over it, for insertion in his General History, to the narratives of others accompanying the Oxford
Map, as allowing easier interpolation of the rescue story, is
fully repelled, I think, by the fact that to this original narra-
tive, thus changed, he signed his own initials, which were not
appended to it before. It is credible, if he meant a fraudulent
interpolation, he would have done what would go far to defeat
his object? On the contrary, these initials recognized his
responsibility for the story he added. But there were obvious
reasons for preferring the "Appendix" to the "Relation."
It was far better composed—far more comprehensive—had
undergone his own as well as Dr. Symond's careful supervision, and was the work of other hands than his, all of them
witnesses and actors in the events they narrated, while the
"True Relation" was evidently scribbled off in a hurry, probably in the very hour of the sailing of the ship. His "Map,
etc.," of 1612 was confined strictly to a description of the
country, and contained none of his personal adventures.

It would thus appear that the incident of his rescue by
Pocahontas in 1607, was first published by him in 1616, and
repeatedly afterwards, and the question arises whether it
should be held true, or, to use the language of Mr. Deane, as
an "embellishment and afterthought"—that is, false and fabulous. It is not likely now that certainty in regard to it can be
attained, and, as little that unanimity of opinion will be arrived at. So various are men's minds, and their ways of
viewing things and actions, that only where there is no room
for doubt, can such unanimity be looked for. A large and
kindlier way of viewing men's acts and motives, and larger
appreciation of the better elements of our nature on the one
hand, and a narrower and less trustful one on the other,
whether derived from nature or from the result of experience
or different individuals, varying infinitely in degree, we see
everywhere around us; and these dispositions, in the absence
of conclusive proofs, will color or shape opinions on all ques-

tions of men's conduct we have occasion to pass upon. Although it be true that these tendencies may, on the one hand, lead to the yielding a too ready credence to marvels that should be relegated to the domain of myth, it is not less so, that on the other, they generate a hypercritical fastidiousness, which as often rejects, as false, what is only rare; and I think it is observable that where this latter tendency exhibits itself in the depreciation of the great and famous, and disparagement of the good, pandering, as it does, to the general vanity, and seeming, by pulling down the high, to lift up the common and the mean, it has a readier acceptance among men, and is harder, for the same reason, to correct and obliterate, even where shown to be unjust, than when the error is in the opposite direction.

In this case, on the broadest concession that Smith gave no publicity to the incident in question, anterior to its appearance in his letter to the Queen, I perceive no sufficient warrant to impeach its truth. When we remember who Smith was, and his career, we seek in vain for an adequate motive for so paltry a fabrication. Did his own fame require it? Was not his whole career one of known and proved adventure, exposure and hairbreadth escapes, of deeds of courage and address, and presence of mind, is well known, real occurrences, done in pursuit of lofty aims, attested and vouched by less questionable proofs and witnesses than history offers, perhaps, in the case of any other hero of that age whom it holds up to our admiration? Were not his certain achievements such as, if unperformed, might have widely changed even the history of the world? Did not the vigor and address with which he ruled alike the colonists and the savages in their first and trying contact, mark him as one of the born rulers of men and events? What worth to him was the *éclat* of figuring in so relatively petty an occurrence? And while we may well believe he desired to say all he justly could do to commend the forlorn Indian girl, cast amid strangers and strange surroundings, to the favor of the Queen and his countrymen, was there not enough, well vouched and known to numbers, of noble and charitable deeds, done by her to save the colony and other lives besides his, of such rare value, as to render most improbable the supposition he would fabricate a story thus alike unneeded for his own fame or for hers? And under what circumstances? He was at the time in high employment by the Plymouth Company, and expecting advancement. Present in London, and cognizant of the falsehood of the story, if false, were Pocahontas and Rolfe, and Uttapotamoy, an old councillor of Powhatan, and who we may fairly presume was present at the scene related by Smith. Could he venture on a palpable falsehood in the presence of so many who knew the facts, and could so easily blast his name and hopes by exposing it, and who, if they did not, must share the shame of it with him? And even if we could believe the last hypothesis admissible, supposing there were none present interested to expose him, does it not become simply incredible when we remember there were numbers of persons then in London, inimical to Smith, delinquents, who had smarted under his discipline in Virginia, and eager for revenge (amongst them doubtless Wingfield, his old and bitter enemy), who would have found means to expose the audacious statement if untrue, and who yet, so far as we can see, left it wholly unchallenged.

Again.—Was not the fact of the absence of the story from all Smith's previous publications, if it were so, though new to us of to-day, patent to all of that day on the appearance of Smith's letter to the Queen? and could it have escaped comment and exposure from the hundreds that must have been familiar with them had it possessed any significance, or demanded any explanations that could not be and were not readily given? Must not it especially have been known and observed by Purchas? and can we suppose its adoption by him into his history, ("Wingfield himself, and his writings being by him,") unless fully satisfied of its truth? Was he so hard run for material that he must press refuted fables knowingly into its pages? and yet what all the world of that day, as far as we are informed, and with all the lights before them, which we have now, seem to have recognized for true, and all the world since, on the faith of that recognition, have accepted as such, shall we now, at the instance, as I think, of a hasty and somewhat presumptuous, quite possibly prejudiced, criticism, reject and discard as false?

Was he not described and praised by the worthiest of those that knew him, and witnessed and shared his labors, as a "God-fearing man," brave, wise and virtuous, and "the freest of all men from the common vices of the time," and of such a man a mere gratuitous fabrication is not predicable or cred-

ible except on the clearest proof? However it may be fashion-
able, in the priggish censoriousness of the day, to sneer at him
as a romancer, I will risk its sneers in stating it as my belief
that no history of travel or adventure of its length can be
found freer from inconsistencies and inaccuracies, capable of
being tested, than that of Smith. It stands to day a substantial monument of truth and trustworthiness, so buttressed by
witnesses and verified by time, in all the greater wonders and
events it records, as to carry our confidence in it also to those
lesser ones it chronicles, where we have less conclusive testimony. The petty specks that microscopic observers have
pointed out in it are all reducible to the tricks of time, memory, and the types, or, of those "optics keen, which see what
is not to be seen." Except to such critics, its mass of truth
swallows up and assimilates such seeming imperfections,
which, like shadows in water, are due only to an imperfect
light.

Smith's defenders are not bound to furnish an explanation
at this late day, even of a plain discrepancy far less of a
merely inferred one. But several might be conjectured in this
case more admissible than a solution that concludes to delib-
erate falsehood. Might not an incident, that looms up to us,
seated in carpeted parlors, as so heroic and romantic in the
distance, have hardly cost Smith, in the presence of the great
objects he was pursuing—the highest man can aim at, the
conversion of the heathen and the founding of a State—of the
many like perils he had escaped, and the dangers that then
hourly encompassed him, more than a passing thought? or
have given it publicity till the time arrived which would
naturally recall it to mind and make the use of it seasonable?
Again, if it had been noticed in his "True Relation," might
not a leaf of it been dropped as it passed from hand to hand,
as is known to have happened to the celebrated "De Imita-
toine," under precisely similar circumstances? Or might not
its mysterious editor have esteemed it one of the matters "fit
to be private," as possibly more calculated to deter emigration
(which it may have been his cue to advance), by showing how
narrowly Smith had escaped death, rather than to further it
by showing his escape from it? Are, still more probably than
all, might not Smith, fresh from a three weeks' painful im-
prisonment, inflicted on a false accusation of aiming to make
himself King of Virginia, have thought it wise to suppress the

incident of this tender intercession for his life by Powhatan's daughter, lest it should receive this preposterous, yet none the less dangerous charge, and again draw him into yet greater trouble than false witness, hate and revenge had already involved him in? Nor should such a surmise be too hastily dismissed as absurd, when we know, as we do, that Rolfe, years after, incurred the marked displeasure of King James, and was actually "appealed as having committed high treason" for having married Pocahontas. Further, no traditions or earlier histories contradict the story. All historians, Virginian, British and American, except Neill, known to me, have accepted it. It is in harmony with man's higher nature and with internal probabilities, as well as with all the uncontested facts come down to us, both of Powhatan and Pocahontas, and, indeed, it, or some such occurrence, is so necessary to account for the extraordinary love and confidence suddenly shown by Pocahontas towards Smith and the Colony, that if this incident were disproved, some other such one would have to be supposed in order to explain them. What is there either wonderful or incredible in the occurrence? Smith had been a captive with the Indians for weeks. Of various knowledge, familiar with dangers, and full of resource, he knew well how to impress with awe the simple savages he had to deal with for dear life. It is unquestionable that he did so impress them, and that they looked on him as a being of some superior, if not supernatural, order.

"*Sicut Dii*," as Strachey quaintly expresses it, was the Indian's estimate of the white man. Why not this young girl's? Yet this very imputed superiority made Smith, their leader, the more dangerous to them. What more natural policy than for their chief to declare forfeit the life that imperilled his and their safety? Or is it at all surprising that a doting father should have yielded to the entreaties of a darling child? What terror was there for her, to render her intercurrence at all incredible, in the uplifted clubs and painted savages which, however frightful to the fancies of the pale-faces, were but playthings to her and the servitors of her will? The true heroism of the act was not in confronting these, but in the tender compassionateness that led her to risk her father's anger (over which she would seem, however, to have well known her power,) and in the exemplifying of that angelic mercy she so often afterwards displayed as to render the re-

jection of it in this one instance alike captious and perverse.
He is but a shallow critic who judges the stories of the past
by the lights of the present. The realities of to-day would be
romance to the men of A. D. 1600. Why not the realities of
that day seem romance to this? What to them would appear
more fantastic and incredible than Thought girdling the
earth in forty hours, or men transported habitually sixty
miles in as many minutes, more than realizing the seven lea-
gue boots, or the deft feats of Ariel, which were the very crea-
tures of fancy of that day? Wherefore, may not the, to us,
romantic stories of Smith or of Pocahontas, be as true as our
more incredible modern achievements would have been to
them? It is absurd to put the printed and published histories
of the seventeenth century in the same category with the
mythic traditions, or MSS., of the Earlier and the Darker
ages. And it seems to me the demand of simple justice to receive such as have long been uncontradicted and not disproved, and are consistent with Nature, as subsantially true.
And especially should this be so, as in the case of Smith,
where the most, if not all the relations received from him,
susceptible of proof, have stood the test, as to have excited
both the surprise and admiration of subsequent historians.

I hardly trust myself in closing these observations to allude
to the section from which the "new lights" I have commented
on mainly come. I fear I may myself be influenced contrary to
my wishes by the unworthiness I might impute. But the old
inherited quarrels of the Puritan and the Cavalier kept alive,
to some extent, in this country by sectional jealousies, have
too often led to mutual unwarranted flings and disparage-
ments to render it necessarily unjust to suppose they may
have had their influence in sharpening and poisoning the
strictures on Smith and Pocahontas—emanating and actively
disseminated, as far as known to me, only from Northern
sources—which I have been engaged in examining. The extra
and special publication of Neill's chapter on "Pocahontas and
her Companions," separate from his general history, at least
shows that my supposition of a spirit at the North ready to
welcome the calumnies and misrepresentations of which it is
full, is not wholly without warrant. Yet all Northern pens
are not thus unjust.

Drake, a specialist in such investigations, at least as dili-
gent as any, and seemingly entirely conscientious, speaks of

"the noble and generous-minded Smith," stating the ground of his praise, cites from him his remark, praying "to be excused" if the account of the plague (in his "Description of New England"), being at "second hand, may not be true in all particulars," and accords to him unqualified faith. The remarkable similarity of all the earlier accounts of the Northern Indians, his inquiries had made him acquainted with, with those of Smith of the Southern—strongly corroborating the truth of both—no doubt much, and justly, contributing to his confidence.

On the whole, the merits ascribed to Pocahontas rest at least on a color of evidence, not contemporaneously contradicted, while the flouts and sneers of late so freely flung on her fame, rest on none, and more probably owe the taint on them to the envy and vulgarity of the sources they flow from, than to the object it is sought to be fastened on.

I believe, then, Smith's story of his rescue by Pocahontas. It might be spared, indeed, as I have said, from the coronal of her fame, and yet leave it one of almost unrivalled lustre. Still, as being one of the brightest and best known of the jewels which compose it, and rounding it off (so to speak) in harmonious completeness, I have thought it should not be yielded up except on clear disproof of her title to it, and not surrendered to the mere inferences only, far short of conclusive, on which it has been demanded, and which seem rather the outgrowth of unfriendly, if not carping, criticism, than demanded by the facts they are deduced from. In giving my reasons for believing it, I have been led into a defence of Smith, which were out of place here, but that though the direct impeachment is of him, the indirect, and obviously no less designed, depreciation is of Pocahontas also. I think both unjust. The little world of us here will pass upon the case, each according to his lights or object. To do so justly and candidly is of more import to us than them. They have already passed to judgment elsewhere, where our praise or blame cannot reach. But for us remains judgment as we judge.

"The old Story of her Alliance with Rolfe"

If meant to imply that she was not married to him, must be held to be a mere unadulterated calumny, aggravated by branding, alike gratuitously, with falsehood the testimony of

Governor Dale, of Secretary Hamor, and the Rev. Alexander Whitaker, than whom are not three more hitherto unimpeached names in all history; and further suppose that not to be the honored wife, but to the tainted mistress of a mere plain English gentleman, were paid those extraordinary attentions which, from the highest circles and most distinguished ornaments of English society, both State and Church, she undoubtedly received.

"The undoubted fact of her Early Lasciviousness"

Not a scintilla of warrant, so far as I am aware, exists to justify this shameful charge. Strachey's phrase, "wanton young girls" imported at that day no tincture of impurity— nor even now would do so, unless required by the context. I might cite hundreds of proofs, but Shakespeare's "little wanton boys, swimming on bladders," and Bacon's "houseful of children, one or two of the eldest respected, and the youngest made wantons!" where the ascription of an impure meaning would desecrate the text, may suffice for instances without further loading the page. Strachey's further *hearsay* statement (necessarily, for he did not arrive in Virginia till 1610, leaving it in 1612, and Pocahontas never once visited Jamestown after Smith's departure for England in 1609 till she was brought a captive there in 1613), that "Pocahontas, Powhatan's daughter, sometymes resorting to our Fort of the age then of 11 or 12 yeares," and "throwing somersaults with the boys in the streets," gives as little countenance to the gross charge, for he further relates that up to that age it was the custom among the Indians for their children to go naked; but "after 12 years they wear a kind of lethern apron and are very shame-faced to be seen." And these are all the grounds known to me to furnish the shadow of support to the accusation. Yet it is on grounds so flimsy and silly, that we find natures gross or malicious enough—some perhaps from mere inconsiderateness—to blow their deflowering breath on a character which, from childhood to the grave, had been perfumed and embalmed for its rare and spotless virtues, by the admiring praise of all that knew her.

"Her Marriage to an Indian"

Is a mere blundering reading of Strachey. The passage is: "They (the Indians) often reported to us that Powhatan had

then lyving 20 sonnes and 10 daughters * * besides young
Pocahonta, a daughter of his, using sometyme to our Fort in
tymes past, of the age then of 11 or 12 years, now married to
a private Captain Kocoum some two yeares since." Strachey
was writing his book in England from 1612 to 1618 or 19, as
shown by internal proofs (it would be too tedious to introduce
here), from notes made by him in 1610-'12, when he was in
Virginia. There are many instances in it of his comments, at
the time he was writing, on transactions which occurred in
Virginia. Here, in referring to the statements of the Indians
made to him in Virginia respecting Pocahontas, he states,
writing it no doubt in 1616 (omitting, as was common at that
day, the proper parenthetic marks), that she was married
two years since to Captain Kocoum, that is, simply, had married Rolfe two years before, *i. e.* 1614, as she really had.
"Kocoum," *per se,* I admit, is a hard nut to crack, but it is
from the same eccentric mint that turned "English" into
"Tassantasses" and "Pocahontas" into "Amonate" without
any known warrant. Mishearing, miswriting, misprinting
or mis-something, undoubtedly, occasioned it, for I hold it
for certain that "Rolfe" was aimed at, however widely missed.

Her charged "Adultery with Rolfe"

Is but the resultant of the careless blunder just exposed, and
may be dismissed with it to the just reprobation so shameful
a charge, unsupported, naturally evokes, with the single remark that if, of old, the swift pursuers of a similar delin-
quency, which seems to have been undenied, were sharply
checked in throwing stones at the offender by Christ Himself,
there seems no rebuke too strong for those whose too fervid
imaginations first invent an uncommitted offence and then
clamorously demand for it the condemnation of the world.

"With John Rolfe"

Alike inexcusable, because alike unsupported, is the similar
charge against Rolfe, a man whose character is vouched, as
we have seen, by Dale, Hamor and Whitaker, men who knew
him, and who held, and were possibly entitled to hold in the
world's esteem, as high a place even, as these modern defam-
ers of his, who did not; but more convincingly still, avouched
as to his high and conscientious honor, his piety, purity and
intelligence, by his own modest and ingenuous letter to Dale;

and as to his most respectable abilities, as well by his letter to
the King and Council, as by their appointment of him to the
second office of importance in the colony.

*"Who was another woman's husband, and her ultimate death
while the wife, so-called, of one Thomas Wrothe."*

Similar loose and careless blundering characterizes both
these statements. "Wrothe," "Wrolfe," "Rolfe," are all but
different readings, by different eyes, of an old and probably
ill-written entry in the Gravesend Register. While the charge
of Rolfe being the husband of Pocahontas, when he was at the
same time the husband of another woman, is founded only, so
far as I can see, on his brother's application for maintenance
of his "Relict and children." What more obviously or reason-
ably removes the fancied difficulty, than to suppose with
Bishop Meade—Pocahontas having died in 1616, and Rolfe in
1622—that he had married again, after Pocahontas's death,
and left a "relict and children" to be cared for?

Some there will always be (whom the light offends), to find
a congenial pleasure in seeking to sully the heroic ideals of the
past, and dim the splendor that encircles every illustrious
name; and tales of calumny, from whatever motive first fab-
ricated, seem far apter to live, and blur a good name, than the
opposite sentiments of love and admiration are to unduly a-
dorn a bad one. Where they are believed unfounded, it is but
due to the dead to confute them, if we can—still more due to
the living, which cannot afford to allow the higher exemplars
of our race to be unjustly pulled down.

This, I think, has been attempted towards Pocahontas. But
I do not allow myself to believe that one who, though a born
barbarian, bore herself according to all known testimony
stainless and beloved in her native woods; modestly and vir-
tuously when in the care and society of the best English blood
that ever came to this country; faultlessly and lovingly as a
wife; and who was received and treated with eminent distinction by the Court, and best people of London, and with such
"civilitie" so carried herself in its society, as to both charm
and surprise it, up to and in the very moment of her death—
shining like a star out of the dark back-ground of her original barbarism, and irradiating her whole career with the
ceaseless glow of charitable deeds—such a one, the better

and purer world will not lightly cease to regard as the "non-pareil," she was reported to be, of her own tribe, but as an honor, also, to her kind.

I append from the Southern Literary Messenger, Richmond, August, 1860, "The marriage of Pocahontas; notes on the date of Pocahontas's marriage and some other incidents of her life." Read before the Virginia Historical and Philosophical Society by Wyndham Robertson, Esq.:

The date of this event, though of little historic importance, yet as a point of history, as well as for other reasons, is not wholly devoid of some curiosity and interest. Although the most incontestible authorities exist whereby to fix it, it is yet singular that an error in regard to it has been so often reproduced as to seem, now, almost imbedded in history. Almost all authorities concur in referring it to *April,* 1613. Stith says "it was in the beginning of April, 1613" (page 130); Beverley says, "Pocahontas being thus married in the year 1613" (page 28); Howison has "1613, early in April;" Sims (page 335), "Spring of 1613;" Hilliard, in Sparks' Biography, "beginning of April, 1613 (Volume II, page 371,) and Campbell, so late as the present year (1860), says "early in April, 1613" (page 109).

Yet it is demonstrable that it took place about the 5th April, 1614.

These writers doubtless reposed on the authority of Smith. But I will show hereafter that he was probably under no mistake, and only seemed to have been by the (probably accidental) misplacing of a marginal note.

About *the time of her capture* there can be no room for mistake. We have the letter of Captain (Sir Samuel) Argall himself, its date, June, 1613, in 4 Purchas, page 1764, *et seq.* It is there stated that he sailed from England "23rd July, 1612"; arrived in Virginia "17th September"; visited Smith's Island "beginning of November"; went to Pembrook river "1st December"; returning to Jamestown "1st January" (necessarily 1613); "arrived at Point Comfort 1st February;" returned to Pembrook river "17th March," thence to Patowameck; captured "Pokahuntis" by treachery; departed with her "13th *April*" for Jamestown, and delivered her to Governor Gates. Again departed in his shallop for discovery "the 1st of May"; returned to his ship "May 12th, 1613" (in margin), and was then, when he wrote, "June, 1613," waiting for a "wind" to go on his "fishing voyage." There is nothing known to me anywhere in conflict with any statement of this letter, but it is entirely in accord with every date and statement come down to us from that period.

We have, then, *the date of Pocahontas's capture* fixed a little before, and her delivery at Jamestown a little after, *the thirteenth April*, 1613. Of course her marriage to Rolfe could not have occurred the *"first," the "fifth," "the beginning," or "early" in April*, 1613.

All agree that she was *"long"* a prisoner before her marriage.

Let us then follow the accounts of her, and learn *how long*. The original authorities (and there could be none higher) are Governor Dale and Ralph Hamor, Secretary of the Colony, and the Rev. Mr. Whitaker. Captain Smith but compiles from them. Dale succeeded Gates as Governor in *February, or March*, 1614, when the latter returned to England, (4 Purchas, page 1773; Stith, page 132), and in a letter, under date of "18th *June*, 1614," sent to England by Captain Argall, (in 4 Purchas, pages 1768-9,) says, "Sir Thomas Gates having embarked himself for England, * * * I put myself into Captain Argall's ship * * and went into Pamunkee river, where Powhatan hath his residence * * with me, I carried his daughter, who had long been prisoner with us." After sundry delays, "came one from Powhatan, who told us * * * that his daughter should be my child, and can dwell with me," &c. He then proceeds:

"Powhatan's daughter I (had) caused to be carefully instructed in the Christian religion, who, after she had made some good progress therein, was, as she desired, baptized, and is since" (*i. e.*, since her baptism,) "married to an English Gentleman," &c.

The marriage, therefore, was, by this authority, between March and June, 1614.

Accordant is Master Whitaker's letter (the Minister at Jamestown), dated also *"Virginia*, 18th *July*, 1614," ("True Discourse," page 59; 4 Purchas, page 1768.) "Sir, The Colonie is much better. Sir Thomas Dale, our * * Governour, * *

hath brought them" (our enemies) "to seeke for Peace of us,
which is made. * * But that which is best, one Pocahontas,
or Matoa, the daughter of Powhatan, is married to an honest
and discreete English gentleman, Master Rolfe, and that after she had openly renounced her country idolatry, professed
the faith of Jesus Christ, and was baptized, which thing Sir
Thomas Dale had laboured a long time to ground in her."

Next, and fullest, is the authority of "Ralphe Hamor, the
younger, late Secretaire in that Colonie," under Dale ("True
Discourse," page 3). Hamor sailed for Virginia, with Sir
Thomas Gates in June, 1609 (4 Purchas, page 1734) ; suffered shipwreck with him on the Bermudas, and arrived out
May, 1610 (4 Purchas, page 1743) ; accompanied Governor
Dale in his expedition to Pamaunkee, March, 1614; was afterwards "employed to Powhatan," May, 1614, (Dale's letter in
4 Purchas, page 1769,) and returned to England with Argall,
June, 1614. His "True Discourse" was written directly after
his return to England. (See his address "To the Reader,"
where he speaks of the Colony as under the command of Governor Gates and Governor Dale "three years and more."
Gates took charge of the Colony in August, 1611.) His account of the capture of Pocahontas is almost absolutely the
same with Argall's own, except a little fuller perhaps, and
except a trivial variation as to the lapse of time, after her
capture, before Powhatan sent in the seven Englishmen (and
which, his writing, as he says he does ("To the Reader,")
"without notes, but in memorie," sufficiently accounts for ; but
which variation only goes still more certainly to fix the marriage after April, 1613.) After stating that a message had
been sent to Powhatan to acquaint him with the capture of
Pocahontas, he proceeds thus: "He (Powhatan) could not,
without long deliberation with his council, * * resolve upon
anything, and * * we heard nothing of him till three months
after * * he sent us seven of our men, * * and word that
whensoever we pleased to deliver his daughter he would give
us satisfaction, * * five hundred bushels of corn, and be forever friends with us. * * We returned his answer * * that
his daughter was very well and kindly intreated, and so
should be however he delt with us, but we could not believe
the rest of our arms were stolen or lost, and till he returned
them all, we would not by any means deliver his daughter.

* * This answer, as it seemed, pleased him not very well, for we heard no more from him till in March last, when, with Captain Argall's ship, * * Sir Thomas Dale * * went up into his own river * * and carried with us his daughter," etc.

Now observe this is written in 1614, just after Hamor's return to England in June of that year. When was that *"March last"* but (according entirely with the date of Governor Dale's expedition, as fixed above by the Governor's own letter) *March, 1614?*

His account proceeds more circumstantially, and more clearly, than Governor Dale's, but in entire accord with it, and is that of an eye-witness, or as he calls himself, *"Ocular testis,"* and as it is at once original and entertaining, as well as curious and rare, I give it in full.

He introduces his "True Discourse" (page 3,) on the "firme Peace that hath been so happily concluded" by "inserting" as "in no whit impertinent" thereto "the endeavors of Captain Argall," viz: his visit to Iapazeus at Pataomecke, and capture there of Pokahuntus—following it with an account of Governor Dale's expedition to, arrival, and proceedings at Pamaunkee, and continues as follows:

"Higher up the river we went, and ancored neere unto the chiefest residence Powhatan had, at a town called Matchcot, where were assembled (which we saw) about 400 men, well appointed with their bowes and arrowes to welcome us; here they dared us to come ashoare, a thing which we purposed before, so ashoare we went, our best landing being up a high steepe hill, which might have given the enemy much advantage against us, but it seemed, they as we, were unwilling to begin, and yet would gladly have been at blowes; being landed, as if they had no show of feare, they stirred not from us, by walked up and downe, by and amongst us, the best of them inquiring for our Weroance or King, with whome they would gladly consult to know the occasion of our coming thither, whereof when they were informed, they made answer that they were there ready to defend themselves, if we pleased to assault them, desiring neverthelesse some small time to dispatch two or three men once more to their King, to know his resolution, which if not answerable to our request in the morning if nothing else but blood would then satisfy us, they would fight with us and thereby determine our quarrell, which was but a further delay to procure time to carrie away their provisions, nevertheless we agreed to this their request, assuring them till the next day by noon, we would not molest, hurt, nor detain any of them, and then before we fought, our Drums and Trumpets should give them warnings, upon which promise of ours, two of Powhatan's sonnes being very desirous to see their sister, who was there present ashoare with us, came unto us, at the sight of whom, and her wellfare, whom they suspected to be worse intreated, though they had often heard the contrary, they much rejoiced, and promised that they would undoubtedly persuade their father to redeem her, and to conclude a firme peace forever with us, and upon this resolution the two brothers with us, retired aboarde, we having first dispatched two Englishmen, Maister John Rolfe and Maister Sparkes to acquaint their Father with the business in hand, the next day being kindly intreated, they returned, not at all admitted Powhatan's presence, but spake with his brother Apachamo, his successor, one who hath already the command of all the people, who likewise promised us his best indeavors to further our just request, and we because the time of the yeere being then Aprill, called us to our business at home to prepare the ground, and set corne for our winter's provision, upon these terms departed, giving them respite till harvest to resolve what was left for them to doe, with this promise, that if finall agreement were not made betwixt us before that time, we would thither return againe and destroy and take away all their corne, burne all the houses upon the river, leave not a fishing weire standing, nor a canoa in any creeke thereabout, and destroy and kill as many of them as we could. Long before this time a gentleman of approved behaviour and honest carriage, Maister John Rolfe had bin in love with Pocahuntas, and she with him, which thing at the instant that we were in parlee with them, myself made knowne to Sir Thomas Dale by a letter from him, whereby he intreated his advise and furtherance in his love, if so it seemed fit to him for the good of the Plantation, and Pocahuntas herselfe, acquainted her brethren therewith, which resolution Sir Thomas Dale wel approving, was the only cause; he was so milde amongst them, who otherwise would not have departed their river without other conditions.

"The bruit of this pretended marriage came soon to Powhatan's knowledge, a thing acceptable to him, as appeared by his sudden consent thereunto, who some ten days after sent an olde oncle of hers, named Opachisco, to give her as his deputy in the church, and two of his sonnes to see the marriage solemnized, which was accordingly done about the fift of April, and ever since we have had friendly commerce and trade, not only with Powhatan himself, but also with his subjects roundabout us; so as now I see no reason why the Colonie should not thrive apace."

These are the only original sources of correct information in regard to the capture, detention, baptism and marriage of Pocahontas, known to me, and, I think, conclusively show that she was kidnapped at Patowomeek in April, 1613, was detained "long" in captivity, was taken to Pamaunkee in March, 1614, brought back to Jamestown about 1st April, was then baptized, and was married to Rolfe "about *the fifth of April*," *one thousand six hundred and fourteen.*

It is, perhaps, of little importance to show how the common mistake originated, but by the light afforded by these *excerpta*, from the original authorities, it is not, I think, difficult. The source of the mistake is probably found in Smith's General History (the edition of 1626 is the one before me), page 113. Smith is reciting from, and *abridging*, Hamor's "True Discourse." The year of Sir Samuel Argall's arrival out in Virginia, is correctly given, in his margin, 1612, but he goes on, *under the same marginal year,* to give an account of Argall's expedition to Patowomeek, and kidnapping of Pocahontas, which, as we have seen above, took place, not in 1612, but in the spring of the *following year,* 1613. There then follows, in Smith (still rewriting and abridging Hamor's "Discourse,") an account of both Argall's and Dale's expeditions, but without the dates, "April 13," of the former, and "March last," of the latter, which fix the years, and opposite the account of the marriage in Smith, is this marginal note.* Now the marginal dates in this compilation from Hamor, have reference to the Treasureship of Sir Thomas Smith, and they are not found in Hamor's work. But the text of the orignal authorities conclusively shows that the

---

"The marriage of Pocahontas to Master John Rolfe, 1613. Sir Thomas Smith, Treasurer.

date just cited—1613—belonged to the commencement of the account of Argall's expedition as given on the previous page of Smith, and was, doubtless, by some accident or inadvertance, printed where we now find it. Seeing the date, 1613, *after the marginal notice of Pocahontas's marriage, and opposite the paragraph in which is the account of it,* with nothing to excite distrust of, and, quite possibly, with no means of collating, the original accounts, and thus correcting the error, our earlier historians naturally adopted the date thus seemingly given by Smith as that of the marriage, and have been followed by later ones, without examination.

The omission by Smith (General History, page 115) of the introductory sentence to Hamor's account of the latter's mission in "May" to Powhatan, has served to seemingly separate, and widely disconnect, the date of the latter event from that of the marriage; and, accordingly, all the histories, while they assign (erroneously as before shown) Pocahontas's marriage to 1613, assign, rightly, Hamor's mission to 1614. That sentence is as follows: "I purposely omitted one thing in the Treatisse of our Concluded Peace, wherewith I intend to conclude my discourse, * * * and this it is." He then proceeds with the account of his visit, as compiled from him in Smith and all the other Histories, and plainly, and inevitably, connects it with the "Peace" of which he has been treating (page 11 *et seq.*), which Peace (the immediate fruit of Pocahontas's marriage) was concluded as above shown recently before the dispatches of Governor Dale and Mr. Whitaker, *June* 18th, 1614. In a word, Hamor's Mission was in the May following the April of Pocahontas's marriage, and immediately before the June of Hamor's return to England, 1614. (See "True Discourse," page 37):

JOHN ROLFE.

John Rolfe is now mainly remembered as the husband of Pocahontas, but was undoubtedly one of the Capital Figures of the great epoch—the first permanent English settlement in North America—with which he is so nearly associated. Yet his name remains almost obscured in history (though all the more imperishable) in the dazzling and never-lessening brightness of that of his Indian Bride, who ever draws off from him the eyes of the world, to that rare Flower of the

Wilderness, which the gardens of civilization hardly rival, and that scion of Nature's nobility, than which the long-descended genealogies of Heraldry offer nothing nobler. But if she doth thus draw off from him the sympathetic regards of all lovers of the good and beautiful, yet do they still often revert, with admiring respect, to one who was quick to see, as he was assiduous to cultivate, the rare worth of the Indian maid, and who, having turned her from Heathendom, boldly faced the prejudices of race, and with the approval of his Government—in the presence of the Governor—of his own countrymen, and of her rude kinsmen of the Forest—in the sight of all men—in the first Christian church erected in the Dominion of Virginia by the ministration of one of the first in time, and not the last in worth, of the pioneers of Christianity in the New World, the Rev. Mr. Whitaker— made her his wife. There are many forms of heroism, and this is one of them. Not secretly, not shame-facedly, but openly, and avowing and recording the high, pure, and loving motives and feelings which actuated him "to sweepe," as he says, "and make cleane the path wherein I walke, from all suspicions and doubts," so that neither present nor after times might justly "taxe or taunt" with "sinister respects alluring him thereunto," he united himself with that noble savage in Christian wedlock.

Quaint, and quite unfashionably made up, Rolfe's letter to the Governor, detailing "the grounds and principall agitations which thus should provoke me to be in love," and asking his approbation, carries with it irresistible internal evidence as well of the scrupulous probity of his principles, as of the singular candor and disinterestedness of his nature, and the heroism of his character. It may be found at large by the curious, in the "True Discourse of the present Estate of Virginia," "written by Ralphe Hamor, the younger, late Secretary in that Colony" (London, 1615), himself an illustrious cotemporary and friend of Rolfe. An extract or two may suffice here:

"Let therefore this, my well advised protestation, which here I make betweene God and my own conscience, be a sufficient witness, at the dreadfull day of judgment (when the secret of all men's harts, shall be opened), to condemne me herein, if my chiefest intent and purpose be not, to strive with all my power of body and minde, in the undertaking of so mightie a matter, no way led (so farre forth as man's weakeness may permit) with the unbridled desire of carnall affection: but for the good of this plantation, for the honour of our countrie, for the glory of God, for my owne salvation, and for the converting to the true knowledge of God and Jesus Christ, an unbeleeving creature, namely, Pocahontas. To whom my hartie and best thoughts are, and have a long time bin so entangled and inthralled in so intricate a laborinth, that I was even awearied to unwinde myself thereout."

He attests further, "*Serena mea conscientia*, the cleereness of my conscience, clean from the filth of impurity, *quo est instar muri ahensi*, which is, unto me, as a brasen wall"; "Nor," adds he, "am I in so desperate an estate, that I regard not what becommeth of mee; nor am I out of hope but one day to see my country, nor so void of friends, nor mean in birth, but there to obtain a mach to my great content."

But if testimony of his high merit, from a less interested source than his own letters, however intrinsically convincing, were yet wanted, it is abundantly furnished. As by that "noble Knight," Sir Thomas Dale, "a man of great knowledge in Divinity, and of a good conscience in all his doings," the wisest and most pious of the earlier Governors of Virginia—(who raised her out of almost the depth of despair, to the "most assured hopes"; placed her peace with the Indians on the firmest basis, and, in great part, through Rolfe's marriage to Pocahontas; and left her in a state of prosperity theretofore unexampled)—who describes Rolfe, in a few strong words, as "an English gentleman of good understanding"—by the reverend and devoted Master Whitaker (sometimes styled the "Apostle of Virginia,") who speaks of him as an honest and discreete English gentleman," and by Hamor, who describes him as "a gentleman worthie of much commendation," with much, besides, to the same effect.

But his title to the highest respectability and consequence in connection with the settlement of Virginia is further shown, and put beyond question, by a historic letter of his to the King, written by him when in London with his wife, Anno 1617, under the name of a Report of the Condition of the Colony when he left it, but containing besides numerous suggestions to his Majesty of such modifications of the Government of Virginia as he deemed calculated to advance and confirm its prosperity. How highly these were esteemed, may be well inferred from the fact that the place of "Secretary and Recorder-General of Virginia" was then first instituted for, and filled by him. At a later period, he was a member of the Governor's Council, which is the latest notice of him, I have met with. Dying in 1622, he left a will, of record, and which is still extant.

In a memoir designed especially to pay due honor to his name,the fact that he was the first of the English Colonists to plant tobacco, would seem such a one as should by no means be overlooked, and the rather that the historical credit of first introducing its culture has been incorrectly asserted for Governor Yeardly by reason of his having, some years later, Anno 1616, recommended the raising of it; and it deserves remark that Yeardly was then residing at Bermuda Hundred, opposite Henrico, where Rolfe lived. Looking to the rapid rise and finally vast dimensions of the trade in it, the man who first applied European skill and energy to the culture of it, would seem, at least, not less worthy to be remembered in history than he who first set a conspicuous example of the use of it. Yet, while all the world knows, from a hundred sources that Raleigh enjoys the latter distinction, few are aware that to Rolfe belongs the former. Yet Hamor, almost the earliest in point of time, and the second of none in point of authority, of the annalists of Virginia (having for his theme the planting of tobacco), signalizes the fact alluded to, and shows his sense of the importance of it, in the following remarkable words: "I may not forget the gentleman, worthie of much commendations, which first tooke the pains to make triall thereof, his name Mr. John Rolfe, Anno Domini 1612, partly for the love he hath a long time borne to it, and partly to raise commoditie to the adventurers in whose behalf, I witness and vouchsafe my testimony, in beliefe that during the time of his aboade there, which draweth near upon six yeares, no man has labored to his power, by good example there, and worthy encouragement into England by his letters than he hath done." It may be truly said, doubtless, that some one else would have set the example if he had not, and not less truly that some one else would, doubtless, have discovered America if Columbus had not. But, I think, we may not, justly, therefore, derogate from the merit of the men who are, actually, the first to open new paths to their kind, of wealth and power. When we consider that tobacco was to Virginia what gold was to Australia—that which alone of their products overbalanced by its rich returns all the disadvantages, dangers and *ennui* of a new settlement, and served still to revive anew hope, fortitude and energy in the breasts of the disappointed and discontented colonists—when we recollect that the colony more than once was reduced to absolute despair, and on the point of being abandoned—may we not safely refer to this new subject of industry, a saving power over its destinies, and justly concede to him, who led the way in apprehending and proving its value, a niche among the benefactors of their race, and, with Smith and Dale, among the true founders of Virginia?

The name Rolfe is Danish, which, softened by the clime, became "Rollo" in Normandy. It first occurs in history about A. D. 600, when Rolf Krake was King of Denmark. [It is worth the parenthesis to repeat, from a Scandanavian writer, that "The graces of his person are said to have equalled those of his mind, and his stature and strength to have been so extraordinary that he was surnamed Krake, an old Danish word expressive of those qualities."] It was brought to England in the person of Rolfe, or Rollo, who accompanied one of the first (I believe the first, but have mislaid my reference) Vykings who overran England. Without seeing reason to claim, or to disclaim, for John Rolfe descent either from the King or the Count, we think he may very fairly be presumed to have sprung from some Danish family (not "a mean one" as he states) of that name, one of the many of that race, who remained permanently in England after the Danish conquest.

From a time lost in the mists of the Past, the Rolfes have resided in the County of Norfolk, where still, on their ancestral possessions, still many reside. From that county and stock John Rolfe emigrated to Virginia.

When I add that so much of further merit was Rolfe's, as to have left a worthy son (noticed below), I have finished the brief memoir intended, *quantum valeat,* to aid in rescuing his name from its too obscure place in history, and said enough, I trust, to vindicate the justness of the remark with which I set out, that John Rolfe was not merely the husband of Pocahontas, but, in truth, one of the capital characters of his time.

Since writing the above, I have met with an interesting ar-

ticle on the Rolfe's, contributed to a Northern Magazine
("Wide Awake," November, 1886,) by Mrs. Raymond Brathwayte, an English lady, which goes to corroborate my own
ideal *prognosis* of the family, and enables me to add some
authentic and interesting facts respecting them. They are
first mentioned in Domesday Book (eleventh century). Of
this special branch there is a record of them as owners of
Heacham, in Norfolk, where they still live, as far back as
1560, and the first entry on it is of the marriage of Eustace
Rolfe and Joanna (Jener), the grandparents of John Rolfe.
I append the registry as given by Mrs. Brathwayte:*

1560. Married Eustacius Rolfe and Joanna Jener, 27th May.
1562. Baptized John, *filius* Eustacius Rolfe, 17th October.
1582. Married Johannes Rolfe and Dorothea Mason, 24th September.
1585. Baptized Eustacius and John, *fille* Johannes Rolfe, 6th May.
1585. Buried Eustacius, *filius* Johannes Rolfe, 2d June.
1591. Baptism, Edwardus, *filius* Johannes Rolfe, 22d February.
1593. Buried Eustacius Rolfe, —— June.
1594. Buried Johannes Rolfe, 1st December.
1594. Married Robertus Redyman and Dorothea Rolfe, 9th March.
1625. Died Robertus Redyman.

We learn from this that John was a twin, born 6th May,
1585, and son of John Rolfe and Dorothea Mason. Agreeing
with Mrs. Brathwayte, to use her words, that it will be "interesting to know the character of the father of him who has
been himself described as an honest and well reputed gentleman." I cite her extracts from "the inscription on brass belonging to his tomb." "It is in Latin. Translated, it runs to

---

*Rolfe is the same name, or most probably of the same origin, as
Ralfe, Ralph, Rolph, and other variations. According to Camden
(*Remaines Concerning Britaine,* page 85, edition 4to., 1637) it is contracted from *Radulph,* and like *Rodulph* signified "Helpe Councill."
Burke (*General Armoury,* edition 1847,) gives us the armorial bearings
of Rolfe of Heacham Hall, County Norfolk, as borne by S. C. E.
Neville Rolfe, of Heacham Hall, Esq., who took the name and arms of
Rolfe by royal license, 19th April, 1837, on coming into the possession
of the property of the late Edward Rolfe, of Heacham Hall, Esq.
Quarterly, first and fourth, gyronny of eight, or and az. on a chief sa.
three amulets, ar.; second and third, gu. five mascles in fesse ar.
within a bordure ar. *Crests*—First, a lion's head erased; second, on
a mount a crescent, therefrom issuant a rose slipped.—*New England
Historical Genealogical Register, April, 1849, page 149.*   R. A. B.

this effect: that he profited his own family much while he remained in life; he wished all his neighbors and relations, through himself, to be of greater worth by helping the poorer with his means. Nothing could be more amiable than he. The reproaches of many he bore, gently bore, without offence of mind." His death occurred very suddenly, in the November of the year following that of his father. In the inscription it is likened "to the extinguishment of a volume of flame by a mass of water, for he was of healthy strength, and when dying had not completed many years (32). His death caused grief to many, but it fared very nobly with him, whom a consciousness of a life well spent, and a record of many good deeds, does not suffer to perish." From the same source we learn that he had to do with the merchant service: "By trading as a merchant, he increased his family estate with the export and import of things which England either abounded with or wanted; he afforded very great service, since, in these matters, he devoted his care and energy." W. R.

FIRST IN DESCENT.

1. THOMAS ROLFE, *b.* 1615; *d.* 16—; *m.* "Jane Poythress;" left issue one child only, a daughter.

Thomas Rolfe was taken charge of, soon after the death of his mother, by his uncle, Henry Rolfe, of London, where, and by whom, he was brought up to manhood. Shortly after, he decided to return to Virginia, where he was born, and did so in 1640. There is little doubt but that he settled there on his patrimonial property. "Varina," near Henricopolis, sixteen miles below Richmond. One, of the two only incidents of his life of which we have any record, strongly confirms this supposition. Both of these incidents are much to his honor, and corroborate the description of him given by the historian Stith, as having been a man of "Fortune and Distinction in the colony." One we give, for its quaintness, in the form in which it is recorded. In Hening's Statute at Large, Volume I, page 327, we find (Act 2), after reciting that the "maintaineing of the fforts, &c., are thought to be of great consequence, in point of honour and security of the colony, any yet of too great burthen of the inhabitants," it is "enacted that the said fortes, with the propriety of a competent quantity of land, be granted to particular undertakers," &c., and proceeds as follows: "And be it further enacted and granted that Left. Thomas Rolfe shall have and enjoy for himselfe and his heires forever ffort James *als* Chickahominy fort, with foure hundred acres of land adjoyning to the same, with all houses and edifices belonging to the said forte, and all boats and ammunition at present belonging to the said ffort: provided that the said Leift. Rolfe doe keepe and maintaine sixe men upon the place duringe the terme and time of three yeares, for which tyme he, the said Leift. Rolfe, for himselfe and the said sixe men, are exempted from publique taxes." (Henricopolis was but a short distance from Chickahominy.) The reposing in him a trust of such importance at that time by the government, and requiring no small resources to execute it sufficiently, attest that he was a man possessing substantial means, brave, loyal, and possessing the public confidence. The other incident recorded of him is the granting him by the Governor, on his petition, of permission to visit his Indian kinsfolk, showing that the manhood, generosity, humanity and superiority to vulgar prejudice or censure, which so pre-eminently distinguished his father, were not dishonored or wanting in his son.

I adopt "Jane Povthress" (not Poyers),* whom he is stated in the "Bolling Memoirs" to have married in England: 1. Because no such name as "Poyers" is anywhere known, so far as I am advised. 2. Because the family of Poythress was already settled in Virginia, and in the immediate neighborhood of Rolfe's residence at Henricopolis (but a few miles below, and on the opposite side of the river)—Francis Poythress appearing as a member of the House of Burgesses, A. D. 1644, for Charles City (then including both sides of James River at those points). 3. Because there is no reference or tradition known of Rolfe having brought a wife with him from England. And 4 Because in a work, "Sandringham," concerning the families of Norfolk, England, and amongst them the Rolfes, the eminent author, Mrs. Herbert Jones, states that Thomas Rolfe came to Virginia when about 20 or 25, and *married there.*   W. R.

---

*Poyers or Pyers, one of the forms of spelling the modern Pierce or Peirce. The third wife of John Rolfe was Jane, daughter of Lieutenant William Poyers, Pyers or Peirce, of Jamestown, Virginia.   R. A. B.

SECOND IN DESCENT.

2. JANE ROLFE, *b.* ——; *d.* 1676; *m.* 1675 Col. Robert Bolling; *b.* 1646; *d.* 1709, and left issue one child only, a son.

Robert Bolling, the first of the name in Virginia, was the son of John and Mary Bolling, of All Hollows, Barkin Parish, Tower Street, London. John was of the Bollings of Bolling Hall, near Bradford, England, who trace back their descent to Robert Bolling, Esquire, who, in the reign of Edward IV, owned that beautiful seat, and who, dying in 1485, was buried in the family vault in Bradford church. His coat of arms is affixed on his tomb, and being the only one in the church, he was presumably the builder or chief benefactor of it. The Robert of this notice came to Virginia in 1660, when not yet fifteen years of age—seems to have early attained to fortune and prominence—and at twenty-nine, married Jane Rolfe. She dying, he married Miss Anne, daughter of Drury Stith. He lived and died at "Kippax," a fine seat on James river, below Petersburg, now in ruins; but his remains were removed thence by a great-grandson (by his second marriage) in 1858, to a mausoleum, erected by the latter in Blandford County. I find no further special notice of Jane Rolfe.

THIRD IN DESCENT

3. JOHN BOLLING, of "Cobbs" (Colonel), *b.* 1676; *d.* 1729 (Member of the House of Burgesses); *m.* Mary Kennon, daughter of Dr. Kennon, of "Conjuror's Neck" (Member of the House of Burgesses), and left issue, one son and five daughters.

Colonel John Bolling settled, lived, and died at "Cobbs," on the Appomattox, below Petersburg. He engaged in commerce, and while conducting an "extensive and gainful trade" with his countrymen, and yet a larger one with the Indians (equally his countrymen), "partook freely at the same time of all the pleasures of society, for which his gay and lively spirit eminently adapted him. Being once, in England, at a feast given him by a kinsman, a Yorkshire lady, hearing him talk, exclaimed in Yorkshire dialect, "Oh, mine Got, you no hear dat man, and he talk English as well as we." "Yes, faith madam, and I hope much better, or I would not talk at all," was his hasty, and not overgallant, reply: "whereat all did laugh merrily."

	Chil-dren	Sons	Daugh-ters

FOURTH IN DESCENT

4. John Bolling (Major), M. H. B., J. P., b. 1700; d. Sept. 6, 1757; m. Aug. 1, 1728, Elizabeth, daughter of Dr. Archibald Blair, and niece of the Commissary James Blair, D. D., founder of William and Mary College, and left issue. [The "Cobbs" family Bible states that Eliz'h (Blair) Bolling m. 2dly —— Bland, and d. April 22, 1775. R. A. B.] (See Notice A) .... — **19** ....

4. Jane Bolling, b. 1703; d. 1766; m. Col. Richard Randolph, of "Curles"; b. 1690; d. 1748 (M. H. B. and Treasurer of Virginia). (See Notice B) .... — **9** | **5** | **4**

4. Mary Bolling, b. 1711; d. ——; m. Col. John Fleming, of "Mount Pleasant" (M. H. B. and Treasurer); b. 1697; d. Nov. 7, 1766, son of Charles Fleming, and grandson of Sir Thos. Fleming, son of Sir John Fleming, 1st Earl of Wigton, Scotland. (See Notice C) .... — **8** | **6** | **2**

4. Elizabeth Bolling, b. 1709; m. Dr. William Gay...... **5** | **2** | **3**
4. Martha Bolling b. 1713; d. Oct. 23, 1749; m., 1727, Thomas Eldridge; d. Dec. 4, 1754 .... **5** | **3** | **2**

4. Anne Bolling, b. ——; d. ——; m. James Murray. (See Notice D) .... **7** | **4** | **3**

FIFTH IN DESCENT

Of John Bollings (4) Children.

5. Thomas Bolling b. July 7, 1735; d. Aug. 7, 1804; J. P., Chesterfield County; m. Elizabeth Gay (5). (See Notice E) .... **10** | **5** | **5**

5. John Bolling, of "Chestnut Grove," b. June 24, 1737; d. 179—; m. Martha Jefferson, sister of President Jefferson. (See Notice F) .... **11** | **6** | **5**

5. Robert Bolling (Col), of "Chellowe," b. Aug. 17, 1738; d. 1769; M. H. B.; m. 1st, Mary Burton, 2d, Susan Watson. (See Notice G) .... **6** | **3** | **3**

5. Mary Bolling, b. July 16, 1744; d. ——; m. 1761; Richard Bland, of Jordan's, b. 1730-1766 (Member H. of B., Continental Congress, and of the Revolutionary Convention of 1774 and 1775), son of the great Richard of Revolutionary fame .... **4** | **2** | **2**

5. Sarah Bolling, b. June 16, 1748; m. John Tazewell of Williamsburg (Judge of the General Court, and

	Chil-dren	Sons	Daugh-ters
Clerk of the Revolutionary Conventions of 1775 and 1776). [Brother of Henry, father of Littleton Waller Tazewell, Governor of Virginia, U. S. Senator, etc. R. A. B.]	7	4	3
5. Archibald Bolling, *b.* March 20, 1750; *d.* ——; *m.* 1st Sarah Cary, 1770, 2d, Feb., 1774, Jane Randolph (6), 3d, Widow Byrd, 1797, 4th, Widow Clark, 1802. (See Notice H)	13	7	6
5. Anne Bolling, *b.* Feb. 7, 1752; *m.* William Dandrige	10	7	3
Of the children of Jane Bolling (4) *wife of Richard Randolph.*			
5. Richard Randolph, M. H. B., *m.* Nancy Meade	13	4	9
5. Brett Randolph, *b.* 1732; *d.* 1759; *m.* Mary Scott in England where he lived and died	5	3	2
5. John Randolph *m.* Frances Bland, *b.* 1752; *d.* 1788; daughter of Richard Bland, of "Cawson's"	4	3	1
5. Mary Randolph, *b.* 1727; *d.* 1781; *m.* Archibald Cary, of "Amphthill," *b.* 1721; *d.* 1787, (Speaker H. of B., Member Convention of 1766, Speaker State Senate)	6	1	5
5. Jane Randolph *m.* Col. Anthony Walke, of "Fairfield," Princess Anne County, M. H. B., son of Anthony and Anne Lee (Armistead) Walke, second in descent from Anthony Voelke, or Walke, from Holland	3	2	1
5. Elizabeth Randolph *m.* Richard Kidder Meade, Aide to General Washington. (See Notice I)	3	1	2
Of the Children of Mary Bolling (4) *wife of Col. John Fleming.*			
5. Thomas Fleming, Captain in Col. William Byrd's Second Virginia regiment in 1758, Colonel Ninth Virginia regiment in the Revolutionary war: *m.* —— Randolph. Killed in battle of Princeton, January 12, 1777	5	1	4
5. John Fleming. Major in the Revolutionary army. Killed at battle of White Plains; unmarried			
5. William Fleming, *b.* July 6, 1736; *d.* February 15, 1824; M. H. B. from Cumberland county; Mem-			

	Chil-dren	Sons	Daughters
ber of Virginia Conventions of 1776 and 1788, and on the Independence Committee of the first; County Lieutenant of Powhatan County, 1776; Member of the House of Delegates of the Old Congress; of the General Court of Virginia, November 25, 1780; of the Court of Appeals, December 24, 1788; President of the Court, 1820-1824; *m.* Elizabeth Champe, daughter of Colonel John Champe, of King George county, Virginia..............	6	1	5
5. Charles, Captain, Seventh Virginia Regiment, and Lieutenant-Colonel in the State Line........................			
5. Mary Fleming *m.* William Bernard........................	10	6	4
5. Caroline Fleming *m.* James Deane...........................	1		1
Of the Children of Elizabeth Bolling (4) *wife of Dr. William Gay.*			
5. William Gay *m.* 1st, Frances Trent, 2d, Judith Scott	13	7	6
5. Elizabeth Gay *m.* Thomas Bolling (5)......................	10	5	5
5. Mary Gay *m.* Neil Buchanan, of Ettrick Banks M. Association, 1770.................................			
Of the Children of Martha Bolling (4) *wife of Thomas Eldridge.*			
5. Jenny Eldridge *b. circa,* 1740................................			
5. Rolfe Eldridge of "Subpœna," *b.* December 29, 1744, Clerk of Buckingham; *m.* Susan Everard Walker	10	4	6
5. Mary Eldridge *b.* March 11th, 174⅔,*m.* Thos. Branch	3	3	
5. Judith Eldridge *b.* March 11, 174⅔ ; *m.* James Ferguson	2	1	1
5. Martha Eldridge *m.* John Harris of England..........	3	1	2
Of the Children of Anne Bolling (4) *wife of James Murray.*			
5. William Murray, *b.* May 6, 1752; *d.* 1815; *m.* Rebecca Bolling (6).............................	10	4	6
5. John Murray, *b.* 1744; *d.* ——; *m.* Susan Yates.......			
5. Anne Murray, *b.* Aug. 30, 1746; *m.* Neil Buchanan	4	1	3
5. Margaret, or Peggy Murray, *b.* February 8, 1748; *m.* Thomas Gordon................	1		1

	Chil-dren	Sons	Daugh-ters
5. Mary Murray, *b.* 1754; *d.* 1823; *m.* 1st, Alexander Gordon, 2d, Col. William Davies. (See Notice J)			
5. James Murray, *b.* 1743; *d.* ——; *m.* Martha Ward.	1		1
SIXTH IN DESCENT			
Of Thomas Bolling's (5) *Children*			
6. Elizabeth Bolling, *b.* 1760; *d.* ——; *m.* William Robertson *b.* 1750; *d.* 1829; Member Council of State. (See Notice K)	13	8	5
6. Rebecca Bolling *m.* William Murray (5)	10	4	6
6. William Bolling (Col. and M. H. D.) *m.* Mary Randolph (6). (See Notice L)	10	4	6
6. Thomas and Mary, deaf mutes, never married. (See Notice M)			
Of John Bolling's (5) *Children*			
6. Martha Bolling *m.* Field Archer	10	5	5
6. John Bolling *m.* —— Kennon	7	2	5
6. Edward Bolling *b.* ——; *d.* 1835; *m.* Dolly Payne	4	4	
6. Archibald Bolling *m.* Catharine Payne	8	6	2
6. Mary Bolling *m.* Edward Archer	1	1	
6. Robert Bolling *m.* Jane Payne	2		2
Of Robert Bolling's (6) *Children.*			
6. Mary Burton Bolling, *b.* 1764; *d.* Aug. 3, 1787; *m.*, November 4, 1781, Robert Bolling, *b.* March 3, 1759, of Petersburg, of the Stith Bollings	3		3
6. Pocahontas Rebecca Bolling *m.* Col. Joseph Cabell, 1782	4		
6. Elizabeth Blair Bolling *m.* Major Thomas West, M. H. D.	4		
6. Linnæus Bolling, *b.* 1773: *d.* 1836, M. H. D.; *m.* Mary Markham. (See Notice N)	4		
6. Powhatan, *b.* 1767; *d.* 1802. (See Notice O)			

	Chil-dren	Sons	Daugh-ters
Of Archibald Bolling's (5) *Children*			
6. Sarah Bolling *m.* 1792, Joseph Cabell Megginson, *b.* 1771; *d.* 1811	5	4	1
6. Anne Everard Bolling *m.* 1st, Sheppard Duval, 2d, Col. Jo. Cabell in 1804		2	
6. Elizabeth Meade Bolling, *b.* ——; *d.* 1823; *m.* 1801 Archibald Robertson (7)			4
6. Blair Bolling, *b.* 1792; *d.* ——; Captain State Guard; *m.* 1st, M. A. Webster 1824, 2d, Penelope Storrs 1827. (See Notice P)	10	5	5
Of Mary Bolling's (5) *Children, wife of Richard Bland*			
6. Richard Bland, *b.* 1762; *d.* 1806; *m.* Susanna, daughter of Ro. Poythress, 4th in descent from Francis Poythress, who came to Va. *circa* 1636	4		
6. Ann P. Bland, *b.* 1765; *d.* ——; *m.* 1st John Morrison, 2d, Peter Woodlief	5	1	4
Of Sarah Bolling's (5) *Children, wife of John Tazewell.*			
6. Elizabeth Tazewell *m.* Samuel Griffin, M. D., M. of Congress 1789 to 1795		1	
6. Littleton Tazewell *m.* Catharine Nevison *née* Boush			1
6. William Tazewell, M. D., *b.* ——; *d.* 1840; *m.* Mary Page Tanner. (See Notice Q)	11	3	8
Of Anne Bolling's (5) *Children, wife of William Dandridge.*			
6. John Dandridge *m.* —— Underwood	1	1	
6. William Dandridge *m.* —— ——	2		
6. Nathaniel West Dandridge, *m.* Martha H. Fontaine (niece of Patrick Henry)	7	4	3
6. Ann Dandridge *m.* Frederick James		1	
6. Jane Butler Dandridge *m.* Rev. Jos. D. Logan	2	1	1
Of Richard Randolph's (5) *Children*			
6. Richard Randolph. Officer of Cavalry, Revolutionary War, *m.* Maria Beverley	8	7	1

	Chil-dren	Sons	Daugh-ters
6. David Meade Randolph, *b.* 1760; *d.* 1830; Officer of Cavalry, Revolutionary War; U. S. Marshal for Virginia; *m.* Molly Randolph (7)	8	6	2
6. Brett Randolph *m.* Lucy Beverley	8	8	....
6. Ryland Randolph *m.* Elizabeth Frayzer	2	1	1
6. Susanna Randolph *m.* Benjamin Harrison, of "Berkeley," M. Non-Importation Association, 1770	1	1	
6. Jane Randolph *m.*, 1774, Archibald Bolling (5)	....	....	....
6. Ann Randolph *m.* Brett Randolph, Jr. (6)	10	8	2
6. Elizabeth Randolph *m.* David Meade	10	8	2
6. Mary Randolph *m.* William Bolling (6) Colonel Cavalry, war of 1812, M. H. D.	5	2	3
6. Sarah Randolph, *m.* William Mewburn	....	1	....
Of Brett Randolph's (5) *Children*			
6. Henry Randolph, *m.* Oct. 7, 1758, Lucy Ward, daughter of Seth and Mary (Goode) Ward	12	4	8
6. Susanna Randolph *m.*, 1783, Dr. Charles Douglass (England) *b.* 1752; *d.* Heir presumptive of the Earl of Morton	5	3	2
6. Brett Randolph, *b.* 1760; *d.* ——; *m.* Anne Randolph (6)	5	4	1
Of John Randolph's (5) *Children*			
6. Richard Randolph, *b.* 1770; *d.* 1796; *m.* Judith daughter of Thos. Mann Randolph, of "Tuckahoe"	3	3	....
6. John Randolph (of Roanoke), *b.* 1773; *d.* 1833; Member of Congress and Minister to Russia. (See Notice R)	....	....	....
Of Mary Randolph's (5) *Children, wife of Archibald Cary.*			
6. Anne Cary *m.* Thom. Mann Randolph, of Tuckahoe	13	6	7
6. Jane Cary *m.* Thomas Isham Randolph, of Dungeness	4	3	1
6. Elizabeth Cary m. Robert Kincaid	5	2	3

	Chil-dren	Sons	Daugh-ters
6. Mary Cary *m.* Carter Page, son of Governor John Page, Major of Cavalry, Revolutionary War........	4	3	1
Of Jane Randolph's (5) *Children, wife of Anthony Walke.*			
6. Rev. Anthony Walke, Protestant Episcopal Church, M. Virginia Convention 1788; *m.* 1st, Ann Mc-Clenahan, 2d, Mrs. Anne Fisher *née* —, 3d, — —	9	6	3
Of Thomas Fleming's (5) *Children*			
6. Mary Fleming *m.* Warner Lewis, of "Warner Hall,"	....	....	....
6. Sukey Fleming *m.* Addison Lewis..................	....	....	....
Of William Fleming's (5) *Children*			
8. Lucy Fleming *m.* John Markham. They went West, and left issue....................	....	....	....
6. Mary Bolling Fleming *m.* Capt. Beverley Chew Stanard, of Spotsylvania county....................	....	....	....
Of Mary Fleming's (5) *Children, wife of William Bernard.*			
6. Daniel Bernard *m.* —— Branch................	2	2	....
Of Caroline Fleming's (5) *Children, wife of James Deane.*			
Of William Gay's (5) *Children, who married Frances Trent and Judith Scott*			
6. William Gay (T.) *m.* Lucy Harrison Coupland (granddaughter of Benjamin Harrison, Signer of the Declaration of Independence)................	10	....	....
6. Elizabeth Gay (T.), *b.* 1772; *d.* ——; *m.* Efford Bentley	9	5	4
6. Thomas Bolling Gay (S.) *m.* Eliza R. Archer........	8	4	4
6. Niel B. Gay (S.) (M. H. D.) *m.* Martha Talley.....	....	....	....
6. Mary B. Gay (S.). *b.* 1794; *d.* 1879; *m.* Gideon A. Strange, M. H. D................	1	1	....
6. Edward Scott Gay. Capt. State Guard, *m.* Catharine N. Tazewell (7)................	....	....	....

	Chil-dren	Sons	Daugh-ters
6. Ann H. Gay (S.) *m.* Charles H. Scott...............	1	1	....
6. Charles S. Gay (S.) *m.* Margaret Erskine, daughter of —— Erskine, M. H. D........................	....	....	....
6. Sally Gay (S.) *m.* James B. Ferguson (6) M. H. D.	8	3	3
Of Elizabeth Gay's (5) *Children, wife of Thomas Bolling* (5). [See Thomas Bolling's (5) children.]			
Of Martha Eldridge's (5) *Children, wife of John Harris.*			
6. Pamela, *b.* 1749; *m.* 1765 Rev. Christopher McRae, Protestant Episcopal Church; issue. For account of him see *Meade's Old Churches and Families of Virginia,* ii., 35-38.............	....	....	....
Of Rolfe Eldridge's (5) *Children, who m. Susanna Everard Walker.*			
6. Rolfe Eldridge (Clerk of Buckingham) *m.* Mary Moseley	10	7	3
6. Susan Eldridge *m.* —— Webber.................	....	....	....
6. Thomas Eldridge *m.* Mary Ayres.............			
6. Courtney Tucker Eldridge *m.* John Williams........	....	....	....
Of the Children of Mary Eldridge (5), *wife of Thomas Branch.*			
6. Bolling Branch *m.* Rebecca Graves.....................	5	3	2
6. Matthew Branch *m.* Martha Cox.................	1	....	1
Of Judith Eldridge's (5) *Children, wife of James Ferguson.*			
6. James B. Ferguson *m.* 1st, Jane Bolling (widow of Robt. Bolling (6), *b.* Payne, 2d, Sally Gay (6)...	8	4	4
Of James Murray's (5) *Children, who m. Martha Ward.* 6. Mary Murray *m.* Edmund Harrison, M. Senate Va.	....	....	....
Of John Murray's (6) *Children, who married Susan Yates.* 6. Elizabeth Murray *m.* Edward Yates................	4	....	....
6. Anne Murray *m.* Jesse Brown................	....	....	....

	Chil-dren	Sons	Daugh-ters
6. Sukey Murray *m.* Theodore Bland Ruffin			
6. James Murray *m.* —— ——.	3		
6. Peggy Murray *m.* —— Elam			
Of Mary Murray's (5) *Children, wife of 1st, Alex. Gordon, 2d, Col. Wm. Davies*			
6. Peggy Gordon *m.* 1st, William Knox, *d.* 1809, 2d, Grief Green, a prominent lawyer of Mecklenburg county	7	5	2
6. Mary Ann Davies *m.*, 1304, Fortescue Whittle, a fellow-exile with Emmet. (See Notice S)	12	9	3
Of Peggy Murray's (5) *Children, wife of Thos. Gordon*			
6. Ann (or Nancy) Gordon *m.* Henry Embry Coleman, M. Va. Sen.	9	5	4
Of Anne Murray's (5) *Children, wife of Niel Buchanan.*			
6. —— Buchanan *m.* —— Cross			
Of William Murray's (5) *Children, who married Rebecca Bolling* (6.)			
6. Anne Murray *m.* Thomas Robinson, an eminent physician and scholar, a refugee about 1800 from the Irish troubles which drove Thos. Addis Emmet and others into exile. Settled in Petersburg, where he died	7	5	2
6. Mary Murray *m.* George Skipwith	7	4	3
6. William Murray *d.* 1866; *m.* Rebecca Skelton	8	1	7

SEVENTH IN DESCENT

Of Rev. Anthony Walke's (6) *sons.*

7. Edwin Walke } by first marriage			
7. David Meade Walke }			
7. John N. Walke, by second marriage			
Of Elizabeth Bollings' (6) *Children, wife of William Robertson.*			
7. Archibald Robertson, *b.* 1772; *d.* 1861; *m.* Elizabeth M. Bolling	4	4	

	Chil-dren	Sons	Daugh-ters
7. Thomas Bolling Roberson, *b.* 1773; *d.* 1828, Sec'y of Territory, 1st M. C., Attorney-General, Governor, U. S. Judge, of Louisiana; *m.* Lelia Skipwith. (See Notice T)			
7. William Robertson, M. H. D., *m.* Christina Williams	7	4	3
7. John Robertson. *b.* 1787; *d.* July 5, 1873; Attorney-General, M. C., Chancellor, (Virginia); *m.* Anne Trent. (See Notice U)	5	2	3
7. Anne Robertson, *m.* Dr. Henry Skipwith, 1813	3	2	1
7. Jane Gay Robertson, b. ——; d. ——; m. John H. Bernard (M. Senate of Va.)	5	1	4
7. Wyndham Robertson, *b.* 1803, M. H. D., M. Council of State, Governor of Virginia, 1836; *m.* Mary F. T. Smith. (See Notice V)	8	3	5

Of Rebecca Bolling's (6) Children, wife of Wm. Murray.

[See William Murray's (5) Children]

Of the Children of William Bolling (6), who married Mary Randolph (6)

7. Anne Meade Bolling, *m.* Jos. K. Weisiger	7	6	1
7. William Albert Bolling, deaf mute, *m.* Eliza Christian	5	3	2
7. Thomas Bolling, *b.* 1807; *m.* Louisa, daughter of Richard Morris of Hanover, M. Va. Con. 1829-30.	5		
7. Jane Rolfe Bolling, *m.* Robert Skipwith (7)			

Of the Children of Martha Bolling (6) wife of Field Archer.

7. Powhatan Archer *m.* —— Walthall

7. Martha Archer *m.* 1st, John Bolling, 2d, ——Berry

7. Ellen Archer *m.* —— Berry

7. Mary Archer *m.* Edward Covington

7. Lucy Archer *m.* —— Archer

Of John Bolling's (6) Children, who married —— Kennon.

7. Evelina Bolling *m.* Alexander Garrett, Clerk of Albemarle county

	Chil- dren	Sons	Daugh- ters
7. Susan Bolling *m*. John Scott.....................................	....	....	....
7. —— —— *m*. —— ——....................................	....	....	....
Of Edward Bolling's (6) *Children, who married Dolly Payne.*			
7. Powhatan Bolling *m*. —— Payne...........................	....	....	....
Of Archibald Bolling's (6) *Children*			
7. Archibald Bolling, *b*. ——; *d*. 1860; *m*. Anne E. Wigginton	4	2	2
7. Edward Bolling, *b*. ——; *d*. 1855; *m*. Anne Cralle	2	1	1
7. Alexander Bolling, *b*. ——; *d*. 1878; *m*. Susan Gray	3	....	3
Of Mary Bolling's (6) *Children, wife of Edward Archer.*			
7. Peter Jefferson Archer *m*. 1st, M. Michaux, 2d, Lucy Gilliam, issue...	....	....	....
Of the Children of Mary Burton Bolling (6), *1st wife of Robert Bolling, of Petersburg*			
7. Mary Burton Augusta Bolling *m*. John Monro Bannister, (Battersea)...	9	3	6
Of Pocahontas Rebecca Bolling's (6) *Children, wife of Col. Joseph Cabell.*			
7. Sophonisba E. Cabell, *b*. 1784; *d*. 1857; *m*. 1809, Robert H. Grayson, son of U. S. Senator William Grayson	10	4	6
7. Sarah Bolling Cabell, *b*. 1786; *d*. ——; *m*., 1805, Elisha Meredith..	9	6	3
.7 Charles J. Cabell, *b*. 1789; *d*. 1810; unmarried. "A notable man in his day." (See Notice W).............	....	....	....
7. Edward Blair Cabell, *b*. 1791; *d*. 1850; *m*., 1812, Harriet Forbes Monroe, a niece of President Monroe	6	3	3
7. Benjamin William S. Cabell, Senate of Virginia, *b*. 1793; *d*. 1862; *m*., 1816, Sarah Eppes Doswell........	10	7	3
7. Mary P. Cabell, *b*. 1798; *d*. 1821; *m*., 1818, Peyton Doswell, *d*. 1820...	2	2	....

	Chil-dren	Sons	Daugh-ters
Of Anne Everard Bolling's (6) *Children, who married 1st, Sheppard Duval, 2d, Col. Joseph Cabell*			
7. Samuel Sheppard Duval............................			
7. Archibald Bolling Duval........................			
7. Jane Randolph Cabell, *b.* 1805; *d.* 1833; *m.*, 1824, Philip T. Allen..............................	4	2	2
7. John B. Cabell, *b.* 1808; *d.* ——; *m.* 1st, 1830, Mary C. Wardlaw; *d.* 1835...............	1	1	
2d, 1839, Martha, daughter of Captain John Posey	3	2	1
7. Elizabeth Robertson Cabell, *b.* 1809; *d.* 1852; *m.* 1st, 1826, James B. Paulett.............	3		3
2d, 1834, Archibald Dixon, U. S. Senator............	7	5	2
7. Robert Bolling Cabell, *b.* 1812; *d.* ——; *m.* 1st, 1833, Anne E. Herndon; *d.* 1834................	1		1
2d, 1835, Eleanor Hart............................	7	1	6
7. George W. Cabell, *b.* 1814; *d.* ——; *m.*, 1837, Mary R. Williams..............................	8	5	3
7. Mary Ann Hopkins Cabell, *b.* 1824; *m.*, 1845, Dr. E. L. Willard (California); issue....................			
Of Elizabeth Blair Bolling's (6) *Children, wife of Th. West.*			
7. —— —— *m.* James S. Jones.................			
7. —— —— *m.* Dr. Joel W. Flood....................		1	1
Of Linnæus Bolling's (6) *Children, who married Mary Markham.*			
7. Mary Bolling *m.* Dr. James Cobbs, brother of Bishop N. H. Cobbs, Protestant Episcopal Church......	1	1	
7. Susan Bolling, *b.* ——; *d.* 1849; *m.* Robert T. Hubard, M. H. D.; lawyer........................	7		
7. Philip A. Bolling, M. H. D. and Judge of Circuit Court, *m.* Mary Eppes............................	1	1	
7. Robert Bolling, *m.* 1st, Sarah Hobson, 2d, Mary Watkins, 3d, Martha Brackett................	4	2	2

	Chil-dren	Sons	Daugh-ters
Of Sarah Bolling's (6) *Children, who married Joseph Cabell Megginson.*			
7. William C. Megginson, *b.* 1794; *d.* 1847; *m.*, 1821, Amanda M. Bocock, sister of Thomas S. Bocock M. C. and Speaker H. of Rep's	11	3	8
7. Elizabeth C. Megginson, *b.* 1796; *d.* ——; *m.* William Berkeley	1	1	....
7. Archibald Bolling Megginson, *b.* 1798; *d.* 1851; *m.* 1st, 1824, Ann R. White; 2d, 1833, Elizabeth Roberts	10	5	5
7. Joseph C. Megginson, M. H. D. Va., Judge in Texas *b.* 1800; *d.* 1858; *m.*, 1826, Almira Montgomery....	2	0	2
7. Samuel B. Megginson, *b.* 1802; *m.*, 1828, Mary A. Johnston	3	2	1
7. Jane Randolph Megginson, *b.* 1804; *d.* ——; *m.* Dr. Nathaniel Powell	2	0	2
7. John R. Megginson, *b.* 1806; *d.* 1875; *m.*, 1835, Mary R. Dunn	3	2	1
7. Benjamin C. Megginson, *b.* 1809; *m.*, 1837, Fanny Blain	9	4	5
Of Elizabeth Meade Bolling's (6) *Children, wife of Archibald Robertson* (7).			
7. Elizabeth Jane, *b.* 1802; *d.* 1822; unmarried	....	....	....
7. Rebecca, *b.* 1803; *d.* 1823	....	....	....
7. Pocahontas Anne, *b.* 1805; *d.* 1838; *m.* —— Bolling	....	....	....
7. Virginia B. Robertson, *b.* 1807; *d.* 1836; *m.* Colonel Ralph Graves	1	1	....
Of Blair Bolling's (6) *Children*			
7. Archibald Bolling *m.* February, 1852, Eliza Trueheart Armistead	5	4	1
7. John Bolling *m.* 1st, October, 1855, Maria Page Armistead, 2d, Julia B. Tinsley	7	4	3
7. Mary Susan Bolling *m.* August, 1851, 1st, Gervas Storrs Burton, 2d, Dr. J. C. Macon	3	1	2
7. Paulina Bolling (?)	....	....	....

	Chil-dren	Sons	Daugh-ters
Of Richard Bland's (6) *Children, who married Susan Poythress.*			
7. Richard Bland *m.* 1st, —— ——, 2d, —— Ledbetter	4	2	2
7. John Bolling Bland *m.* 1st, ——Eppes, 2d, Rachel Reed, 3d, E. Cargill	5	3	2
7. Sarah Bland *m.* Thomas Bott	3	2	1
7. Theodorick Bland *m.* Mary Harrison	5	1	4
7. Mary Bland *m.* Elgin Russell	....	....	....
Of the Children of Anna P. Bland (6) *wife of, 1st, I. Morrison, 2d, P. Woodlief.*			
7. Hannah Woodlief *m.* Dr. Hardaway	1	1	....
7. Anna Woodlief *m.* —— Jeffrey	2	2	....
7. Elizabeth Woodlief *m.* Dr. Shadrach Alfriend	4	3	1
Of Littleton Tazewell's (6) *Children, who married Catharine Nevison.* 7. Sarah Bolling Tazewell *m.* William O. Goode, M. C.	....	....	....
Of Wm. Tazewell's (6) *Children, who m. Page Tanner.*			
7. Willianna Blair Tazewell	....	....	....
7. Catharine Nevison Tazewell *m.* 1st, E. Ambler, 2d, Capt. Ed. S. Gay (6), Va. State Guard	7	1	6
7. Henrietta Watkins Tazewell *m.* C. I. Fox, Agent Associated Press	3	3	....
7. Mary Louisa Tazewell *m.* Dr. J. B. Southall	1	....	1
7. Sally Bolling Tazewell *m.* Dr. George Fitzgerald	4	2	2
7. Martha Jefferson Tazewell *m.*, after her sister's death, Dr. J. B. Southall	....	....	....
7. Jane Rebecca Tazewell	....	....	....
7. Nancy Rosalie Tazewell *m.* Andrew L. Ellett	4	2	2
7. Isabella Tazewell	....	....	....
Of John Dandridge's (6) *Children, who m.* —— *Underwood.* 7. Bolling Dandridge *m.* ——	1	1	....

	Chil-dren	Sons	Daugh-ters
Of Nathaniel West Dandridge's (6) *Children.*			
7. Charles F. Dandridge *m.* —— McGhee			
7. William F. Dandridge *m.* —— Stith			
7. Anna Dandridge *m.* W. Hereford			
7. Martha Dandridge *m.* R. Bolton			
7. Nathaniel West Dandridge *m.* H. Wylie			
7. Rosalie Dandridge *m.* W. D. Bradford			
Of William Dandridge's (6) *Children, who m.* —— *Stith.* 7.			
Of Anne Dandridge's (6) *Children, who married F. James.* 7. —— *m.* —— Utz, Fincastle	1	1	
Of the Children of Jane Butler Dandridge (6) *and Rev. Jos. D. Logan*			
7. James W. Logan *m.* S. W. Strother			
Of Richard Randolph's (6) *Children, who m.* ——			
7. Robert B. Randolph (Lieut. U. S. Navy) *m.* Maria Beverly	5	1	4
7. Wm. Randolph, Mid. U. S. Navy (on board Chesapeake when taken—lost in the Wasp)			
7. Maria B. Randolph *m.* Philip Duval	5	4	1
Of David Meade Randolph's (6) *Children.*			
7. Wm. B. Randolph *m.* Sarah Lingan	10	4	6
Of Brett Randolph's (6) *Children, who m. Lucy Beverley.* 7. Edward Randolph (Capt. U. S. A.) *m.* Bland Beverly	1		1
7. Carter Beverley Randolph (Ass't Surgeon U. S. N.) Anne Tayloe Farrar (*b.* Beverly)	6	2	4
7. Victor Moreau Randolph (Capt. U. S. N. and C. S. N.) *m.* Augusta Granberry	3	3	
7. Franklin Randolph *m.* Ann Corbin of "The Reeds"	2	2	

	Chil-dren	Sons	Daugh-ters
7. Theodric Randolph *m.* —— Brand............................	1	....	1
Of Ryland Randolph's (6) *Children, who married Elizabeth Frazier.*			
7. —— *m.* ——..	1	1	....
7. —— *m.* ——..	1	....	1
Of Susan Randolph's (6) *Children, wife of Benj'n Harrison, of "Berkeley"*			
7. Benjamin Harrison *m.* 1st, —— Mercer, 2d, Page	....	....	....
Of Jane Randolph's (6) *Children, wife of Archibald Bolling* (5)			
[See Archibald Bolling's (5) Children]			
Of Ann Randolph's (6) *Children, wife of Brett Randolph, Jr.* (6).			
7. Kidder Randolph *m.* Betsey Montague.................	....	....	....
7. Howard Randolph *m.* Meads (Kentucky)................	....	....	....
7. Anne Randolph *m.* Joseph Michaux.....................	....	....	....
7. Susan Randolph *m.* Frank Watkins.......................	....	....	....
7. Brett, and Patrick, twins....................................	....	....	....
Of Elizabeth Randolph's (6) *Children, wife of David Meade.*			
7. John E. Meade, *b.* 179–; *d.* 1854; *m.* Rebecca Beverley	6	2	4
7. Charlotte Meade, *b.* 179–; *m.* Dr. J. Y. Stockdell....	11	5	6
7. Rebecca Meade, *b.* 180–; *m.* James Lea.................	6	3	3
Of Mary Randolph's (6) *Children, wife of William Bolling* (6).			
[See Wm. Bolling's (6) Children.]			

Of Henry Randolph's (6) *Children, who married Lucy Ward.*
7. Henry Randolph, of "Warwick," *b.* 1784; *d.* October 26, 1840; *m.* 1st, Caroline Matilda, daughter of Major Smith, of Manchester, Virginia; *d.* Sept. 25, 1808, without issue, 2d, Eliza Griffin Norman,

	Chil-dren	Sons	Daugh-ters
of a Henrico family from Pennsylvania and of the Society of Friends, 3d, Mrs. Perry, a descendant of Thomas Tinsley, planter, who emigrated to Virginia from Yorkshire, England, near the close of the seventeenth century...	10	6	4
7. Mary Randolph *m.* 1st, Geo. Thornton, 2d, James Maury	7	4	3
7. Brett Randolph..	....	....	....
7. Catharine Cochrane Randolph, *b.* 1797; *d.* Dec. 12, 1852; *m.* Josiah Bartlett Abbot, of "High Meadow," Henrico county, *b.* in Connecticut June 1, 1793; *d.* Sept. 23, 1849............................	2	1	1
7. Susan Frances Randolph *m.* Alex'r Lawson Botts, *b.* 1800 (M. Council of State) and brother of Hon. John Minor Botts..	10	6	4
Of Susanna Randolph's (6) *Children, wife of Dr. Douglass.*			
7. Susan Mary Ann Douglass, *b.* 1785; *m.* 1st, Wallace, 2d, 1808, Capt. John Tucker, of Island of Bermuda	4	2	2
7. Charles Brett Douglass.............. ⎫			
⎬ twins; *b.* 1789....	....	....	....
7. Archibald Aberdeen Douglass.. ⎭			
7. Heartly Douglass, *b.* 1786................................	....	....	....
7. Eliza Randolph Douglass, *b.* 1791............................	....	....	....
Of Brett Randolph's (6) *Children.*			
[See Anne Randolph's (6) Children.]			
Of Richard Randolph's (6) *Children.*			
7. Tudor	....	....	....
7. St. George, a deaf mute...........................	....	....	....
7. —— ——.................................	....	....	....
Of Anne Cary's (6) *Children, wife of Thos. Mann Randolph, of Tuckahoe*			
7. Mary Randolph *m.* David Meade Randolph (6)	8	6	2

	Chil-dren	Sons	Daugh-ters
7. Elizabeth Randolph *m.* Robt. Pleasants, of "Four-mile Run," 4th in descent from John Pleasants from Norwich, England, in 1665, in his 25th year	5	1	4
7. Thos. Mann Randolph, of "Edge Hill," *b.* 1764; *d.* 1836 (Governor of Virginia, M. H. of R.) ;*m.* Martha (daughter of President) Jefferson.................	12	5	7
7. Wm. Randolph *m.* Lucy (daughter of Gov. Beverley) Randolph	3	2	1
7. Judith Randolph *m.* Richard Randolph, of "Bizarre" (6).................................	3	3	....
7. Ann Cary Randolph *m.* Gouverneur Morris (N. York), Minister to France 1792-94....................	1	1	....
7. Jane Randolph *m.* Thos. Esten Randolph...............	8	4	4
7. John Randolph, M. D., *m.* Judith Lewis....................	4	3	1
7. Harriet Randolph *m.* Rich'd S. Hackley, Consul at Cadiz	4	1	3
7. Virginia Randolph *m.* Wilson J. Cary.....................	6	2	4
Of Jane Cary's (6) *Children, wife of Thos. Isham Randolph.*			
7. Archibald Cary Randolph *m.* Lucy Burwell, of "Carter Hall".................................	7	3	4
7. Thomas Randolph (twin of Isham) *m.* 1st, Mary Skipwith, 2d Catharine Lawrence. Killed in the battle of Tippecanoe..............................	2	....	2
7. Isham Randolph (twin of Thomas) *m.* Ann R. Coupland	12	4	8
7. Mary Randolph *m.* Randolph Harrison, of "Clifton"	13	5	8
Of Elizabeth Cary's (6) *Children, wife of Robt. Kincaid.*			
7. Mary J. Kincaid *m.* Charles Irving.....................	8	5	3
Of Mary Cary's (6) *Children, wife of Carter Page*			
7. John Cary Page *m.* Mary A. Trent.............................	12	5	7
7. Henry Page *m.* —— Deane...........................	8	4	4
7. Mann Page, M. D., *m.* Jane Walker.....................	12	8	4
7. Mary Page lost her life in the burning of the Richmond Theatre, Dec. 26, 1811....................	....	....	....

	Chil-dren	Sons	Daugh-ters
Of Anthony Walke's (6) Children.			
7. Anthony Walke *m.* 1st, Jane Ritson, 2d, Ann Livingston	5	3	2
7. Edwin Walke *m.* Sarah Massenburg	5	2	3
7. Susan M. Walke *m.* Chas. H. Shield	4	2	2
7. John N. Walke *m.* 1st, —— Land, 2d, Anna M. Baylor	2	1	1
7. Jane E. Walke *m.* Richard Watson	....	....	....
Of the Children of Mary Fleming (6) 2d wife of Warner Lewis.			
7. Julia Lewis *m.* Thomas Throckmorton, of Williamsburg, Va.	....	....	....
7. John Lewis *m.* Eleanor Lewis (his cousin)	....	....	....
Of the Children of Sukey Fleming (6) who married Addison Lewis.			
7. Susan Lewis *m.* William Byrd, of "Westover," (?)	2	2	4
Of the Children of John Markham, who married Lucy Fleming.			
7. Descendants in the West	....	....	....
Of the Children of Beverley C. Stanard, who married Mary Bolling Fleming.			
7. Eliza J. F. Stanard *m.* Samuel O. Eggleston	1	1	....
7. John C. Stanard *m.* Sarah T. Thurston	7	3	4
7. Julia A. V. Stanard *m.* Dr. A. L. Woodridge	3	1	2
Of the Children of Daniel Bernard (6), who married —— Branch.			
7. Cyrus Bernard (Mid. U. S. Navy) prisoner of war at Algiers, killed in a duel at Havana, May 15, 1821	....	....	....
7. Christopher Bernard, Sergeant of Richmond volunteers (war of 1812), grandfather of the late Cyrus A. Branch, M. Va. S. and prominent lawyer of James City county; *m.* ——; left issue	....	....	....

	Chil-dren	Sons	Daugh-ters
Of Thomas Bolling Gay's (6) *Children*			
7. Ellen Gay *m.* Jacob Skein	2	1	1
7. Delia Gay			
7. William Gay *m.* —— Jackson	5		5
7. Eliza S. Gay			
7. Powhatan A. Gay			
7. Virginia F. Gay			
7. Bolling Gay, C.S.A., died at Camp Douglass April 1865			
Of the Children of Elizabeth Gay (6) *wife of Edward Bentley.*			
7. Eliza Gay Bentley *m.* Daniel Harris			
7. Wm. Field Bentley *m.* Sarah Dupree		2	
7. Fanny Trent Bentley *m.* Wm. Houston			
7. Efford Bolling Bentley *m.* Lucy W. Chamberlayne, daughter of Prof. Lewis W. Chamberlayne, M.D.			
7. John Gay Bentley *m.* Judith Thompson			
7. Maria Buchanan Bentley *m.* Daniel B. Friend			
7. Alex'r Willis Bentley, M. D., *m.* —— Peters			
7. Lavinia Bentley *m.* William Roper			
Of William Gay's (6) *Children*			
7. Peterfield Gay, M. D., *m.* —— Christian	4		4
7. B. Franklin Gay *m.* —— Baptist	7	5	2
Of Neil B. Gay's (6) *Children*			
7. William Gay *m.* Sarah Bruce			
7. Neil B. Gay *m.* Mary Bunn	6	4	2
7. Martha Gay *m.* —— Perkins	1	1	
7. Pocahontas V.			
7. Ann Caroline			

	Chil-dren	Sons	Daugh-ters
Of Sally Gay's (6) *Children, wife of James B. Ferguson.*			
7. Judith Gay Ferguson *m.* J. A. Carr	1	1	....
7. Pocahontas Ferguson *m.* J. M. Vaughan	5	2	3
7. James B. Ferguson *m.* Emma C., daughter of Colonel John Henry, and grand-daughter of Patrick Henry, the Orator	2	1	1
7. Mary Francis Ferguson	......	......	....
7. William Gay Ferguson *m.* Margaret Bryce, *née* Pickett	2	1	1
Of Edward S. Gay's (6) *Children*			
7. Matoaca Gay, a distinguished society writer, under the *nom de plume* of "Bric-a-Brac"	......	......	....
7. Louisa Gay *m.* Robert C. White	......	......	....
7. Edwd. S. Gay *m.* Sarah Ewell	......	......	....
7. Carolina Gay *m.* Charles P. Winston; *d.* January 1, 1887	......	......	....
7. Minnie W. Gay	......	......	....
Of Mary B. Gay's (6) *Children, wife of Gideon A. Strange.*			
7. William Gay Strange	......	......	....
Of Charles S. Gay's (6) *Children.*			
7. Charles Wyndham Gay, C. S. A., killed in battle	......	......	....
7. Henry Erskine Gay	......	......	....
7. Frances B. Gay *m.* 1875, R. H. Catlett; issue	......	......	....
7. Lizzie E. Gay	......	......	....
7. William Gay	......	......	....
7. Agatha Estell Gay	......	......	....
7. Caroline Scott Gay *m.* W. M. Allen	......	......	....

	Chil-dren	Sons	Daugh-ters
Of Rolfe Eldridge's (6) *Children, who married Mary Moseley.*			
7. Susanna Eldridge *m.* Dr. James Austin..................			
7. Lucy Eldridge *m.* Rev. James Fitzgerald.................			
7. Elizabeth Eldridge *m.* B. Austin............................			
7. Delia Eldridge *m.* Robert Kincaid Irving, M. Sen. Va., Clerk of Buckingham county; issue................			
7. William Eldridge *m.* —— Nixon................			
7. Mildred Kidder Eldridge *m.* Wm. M. Cabell............			
7. Benjamin Eldridge *m.* Eliz. Perkins................			
7. John Eldridge *m.* Sarah Moseley............................			
7. Frances Eldridge *m.* Samuel A. Glover; issue..........			
Of the Children of Susan Eldridge (6), *who married —— Webber.*			
7. Thomas *m.* Mary Ayres............................			
7. Courtney T. Eldridge *m.* Jno. Williams................			
Of Bolling Branch's (6) *Children, who married Rebecca Graves.*			
7. Mary Susan Branch *m.* John F. Wiley, M. Council of State and Lieutenant-Governor of Virginia......	9	6	3
7. William Branch *m.* —— ——			
7. Sally Branch *m.* Captain Edw'd Gregg................			
Of Matthew Branch's (6) *Children, who married Martha Cox.*			
7. Polly Branch *m.* Thomas May............................			
Of James B. Ferguson's (6) *Children, who married 1st, Jane Bolling, born Payne, 2d, Sally Gay* (6).			
7. Jane Elvira Ferguson *m.* Peachy R. Grattan, Reporter of the Court of Appeals............	10	2	8
[For his other children see Sally Gay's (6) children.]			

	Chil- dren	Sons'	Daugh- ters

Of Elizabeth Murray's (6) *Children, wife of Edward Yates.*

7. Mary Yates *m.* William Hamlin...........................

7. Elizabeth Yates...........................

Of Margaret, or Nancy Murray's (6) *Children, wife of Thomas Gordon*

7. Nancy *m.* Henry Embry Coleman, Virginia Senate; issue...........................

Of Peggy Gordon's (6) *Children, wife of 1st, William Knox, 2d, Grief Green*

7. Mary Ann Knox *m.* Dr. Thomas Goode.....................	8	2	6
7. Sophia Knox *m.* John Buford..................................	2		
7. John F. O. Knox, M. H. of D. of Va..........................			
7. Henry Green..			

Of Mary Ann Davies' Children (6), *wife of Fortescue Whittle.*

7. Wm. Conway Whittle, Commander U. S. N., afterwards Commodore C. S. N., *m.* Elizabeth Sinclair, daughter of Com. W. Sinclair, U. S. N.................	10	5	5
7. Fortescue Whittle...			
7. James M. Whittle, M. Va. Convention 1850; Sen. Va. *m.* 1st, Mary Coles, 2d, Cornelia L. Skipwith (7)....	2		2
7. Conway D. Whittle *m.* Gilberta Sinclair, daughter of Com. W. Sinclair, U. S. N.................................			
7. John S. Whittle, Surgeon U. S. N.; *m.* 1st, Jane Patterson, 2d, Anne Southgate.................................	1	1	
7. Lewis Neale Whittle *m.* Sarah M. Powers.............	12	5	7
7. Stephen Decatur Whittle, Secretary in Virginia State Convention 1849-'50, *m.* Nannie, daughter of George Taylor, and grand-daughter of the far-famed John Taylor of "Hazlewood," Caroline county, Virginia; United States Senator; author of various able works on Agriculture, Political Economy, etc., under the *nom de plume* of "Arator"	4	1	3

	Chil-dren	Sons	Daugh-ters
7. Francis McNeece Whittle, Bishop of the Protestant Episcopal Diocese of Virginia, *m.* Emily Fairfax (See Notice S)			
7. Powhatan Bolling Whittle, Colonel C. S. Army			
Of —— Buchanan's (6) *Children, wife of —— Cross.*			
7. ——Cross *m.* Robert Yuillee; left issue			
Of Anne Murray's (6) *Children, wife of Dr. Thomas Robinson.*			
7. William Murray Robinson, a rarely accomplished *amateur* in Art and Literature, *b.* 1807; *d.* 1878; *m.* Sarah A. Mills; issue	3	2	1
7. Robert Emmett Robinson, M. D., *b.* ——; *d.* 1865; *m.* 1st, Adeline Dewees, of Philadelphia, 2d, Indiana Henley, 3d, Virginia E. Stainback	2	1	1
7. Powhatan Robinson *m.* Anne Eason			
Of Mary Murray's (6) *Children, wife of George Skipwith.*			
7. Robert Skipwith *m.* 1st, Jane Rolfe Bolling (7), 2d Eliz. Bolling			
7. William M. Skipwith			
7. George N. Skipwith, M. D., *m.* Maria L. Brooks			
7. Cornelia Lotte Skipwith *m.* James M. Whittle (7)	1		1
7. Thomas Bolling Skipwith, *b.* ——; *d.* 1873; *m.* Emma Darrieux	1	1	
Of William Murray's (6) *Children*			
7. Rebecca B. Murray			
7. Matoaca Murray *m.* C. L. Gifford, Newark, N. J.	3	2	1
7. Nannie S. Murray *m.* Dr. J. B. Wiley (8)	5	2	3
7. Louisa S. Murray			
7. Mary Murray			
7. Cornelia S. Murray			
7. Gay Bernard Murray *m.* Lewis E. Rawlins	3	1	2

	Chil-dren	Sons	Daugh-ters
Of Ann Gordon's (6) Children, wife of Henry E. Coleman.			
7. Elizabeth Ann Coleman *m.* Charles Baskerville......	4	3	1
7. Mary Margaret Coleman *m.* Richard Logan (Member Senate Virginia)...............	9	5	4
7. John Coleman *m.* 1st, Elizabeth Clark, 2d, Mary Love	....	....	....
7. Thomas Gordon Coleman (Member House Delegates) *m.* Anne Clarke...............	5	3	2
7. Henrietta Maria Coleman *m.* Rev. John Clarke....	3	2	1
7. Henry E. Coleman (Member House Delegates) *m.* Mary Turner...............	....	....	....
7. Ethelbert Algernon Coleman, M. D., *m.* 1st, Elizabeth Sims, 2d, Fanny Ragsdale...............	....	....	....
7. Sarah Coleman *m.* David Chalmers (Member House Delegates)	....	....	....
7. Charles Coleman *m.* 1st, Sarah Eaton, 2d, Alice Sydnor	...2	1	1
7. Jane C. Coleman *m.* Charles E. Hamilton...............	....	....	....

APPENDIX.

NOTICE A.

Major JOHN BOLLING[4] inherited his father's love of pleasure and his business qualifications, but without his appetence for trade. His energy and sagacity showed themselves in long, and in those days perilous, journeys through a wilderness country and the judicious choice of valuable, unappropriated lands, with which he afterwards richly endowed his large family. He was "fond of fine Horses, Hounds, Hunting, Fishing, Fowling, Feasting and Dancing, yet doted on his wife and children," was of an even temperance in all things as well as of an admirable vein of humor—public-spirited, hospitable and popular. He was "County-Lieutenant" of Chesterfield, an office of much dignity and importance in those days, and as such commanded the militia, and presided over its Courts. He, also, for thirty years, represented his county in the House of Burgesses, living (as Wynne has it) "in a style of elegance and profusion not inferior to the Barons of England, and dispensing a hospitality which more than half a century of sub-division, exhaustion and decay has not entirely effaced from the memory" or divorced from the practice, of many of his numerous descendants.

NOTICE B.

JANE BOLLING[4] was the mother of John Randolph, the father of the celebrated John, of Roanoke, and her husband of that stock, which Wynne says "may be pronounced the most distinguished in the History of the Colony and the Commonwealth of Virginia;" a judgment which none will dissent

from on learning that Thomas Jefferson and John Marshall
were of it. They are too conspicuous in all the histories of
Virginia to demand here any but the most cursory notice.
The patriarch of the family was William Randolph, who came
from Yorkshire, in England, to Virginia in 1660. He was
soon enabled to buy the magnificent property of "Turkey Island," thirty miles above Jamestown, where he permanently
settled. He married Mary Isham, daughter of Henry and
Katharine Isham, of the family of Ishams of Northampton-
shire, England, who bore him many children, but his worldly
fortunes kept full pace with his progeny, all of whom he settled around him on fine estates, and left rich. They, too, were
distinguished for energy, talents and success, and achieved,
with still expanding families, still enlarging possessions. The
Randolphs have filled, for a long course of years, some or
others of the very highest political trusts—Colonial, State
and Federal. Numbers, and free living, at length supervened
on wealth, so that at the end of a century "none of the name,"
says Bishop Meade, "owns a rood of those immense tracts of
land on which their fathers once lived." But the prestige of
the name long survived its fortunes, so that when an ambit-
ious mother was once twitted for marrying her daughter to a
poor Randolph, she sharply answered, that "an ounce of Randolph was worth a pound of gold." And many still live who
maintain the credit and distinction of the name.

NOTICE C.

MARY BOLLING[4] we know of only as introducing into her
family that of the FLEMINGS. I learn from one of them that
they were of Flemish descent, one of whom, a man of high
rank, is said to have settled in Scotland in the reign of David
I. But the *propositus* to whom it can be clearly traced was
Sir Malcolm Fleming, Sheriff of Dumbarton under Alexander
III. From him Sir Thomas, the progenitor of the Virginia
family, second son of the first Earl of Wigton, traces his descent through a line of singularly distinguished ancestors, successively occupying the most prominent positions. They were
friends of the Bruce, and favorites of successive kings, as
well as it seems of the people of Scotland also, forming the
most illustrious connections, and attaining finally to the rank
and title of Earls of Wigton. Of the founder of the Virginia

branch (Sir Thomas, who emigrated in 1616), Colonel John Fleming, who married Mary Bolling, was a grandson. Many of the name in Virginia have done honor to their lineage. A Miss Fleming of this family (citing from their genealogy kindly communicated by one of the descendants) married Thomas Randolph, of Tuckahoe. A Tarleton Fleming married Mary, daughter of Edmund and Judith (Randolph) Berkeley, of "Barn Elms." Anne,[15] granddaughter of Sir Thomas,[13] married John Payne, an English gentleman of wealth and education, who settled in the county of Goochland. They had issue: 1. John,[16] who married Mary, daughter of William and Lucy (Winston) Coles, and had issue, 1. Walter[17]; 2. William Temple; 3. Isaac, who all died unmarried; 4. Dorothea, who married 1st, John Todd, a lawyer of Philadelphia, and 2d, James Madison, President of the United States; 5. Lucy[17] married 1st, George Steptoe Washington, nephew of General Washington, 2d, Thomas Todd, Justice Supreme Court of the United States; 6. Anne, married Richard Cutts, Member of Congress from Maine. Her granddaughter, Adele,[19] married 1st, United States Senator Stephen A. Douglas, 2d, General Robert Williams, United States Army; 7. Mary[17] married J. G. Jackson, Member of Congress from Virginia, a cousin of General T. J. (Stonewall) Jackson, Confederate States Army; 8. John, married Clarissa Willard and went to Kentucky.

NOTICE D.

ANNE BOLLING[4] lived to a great age and was of the large stature, high courage, and awe-inspiring bearing of her great Indian progenitor, Powhatan, as the following tradition of her well attests. Sojourning with a kinswoman, whose house was being rifled by Tarleton's soldiers, she said, "Betsy, can you sit still and allow yourself to be plundered this way"? then going up to the commander of the party with arms akimbo, she thus accosted him: "Take off your drunken gang, sir, this minute, or I will fetch a squad from Tarleton will teach you how to behave in a gentleman's house." "Come, boys," said the officer, "let's be off, this woman's tongue is sharper than Tarleton's sword;" and off they went at once faster than they came. Her husband, James Murray, was of the ancient family and Clan of that name, of which the Dukes

of Athol were the chiefs. Chief-Justice Mansfield was among
its distinguished members. They had fallen into decay about
this time, as Lord Campbell's life of him shows. The habits
of the family in Virginia were not such as to build up their
fortunes anew. Eminently free from all vices, they sympa-
thized with all who suffered, were unbounded in their liber-
ality and lavishly hospitable. The son of James—William—
was, from a distinguished stateliness, yet engaging simplicity of carriage, lovingly called the "old Duke." In his family
I was at a second home, and surely if there ever was one over
which the Spirits of Benevolence, Hospitality, Loving-kind-
ness and Unselfishness poured unstinted their sweet influen-
ces, it was this.

NOTICE E.

THOMAS BOLLING[5] and ELIZABETH GAY.[5]—These, my
grandparents, were first cousins, and reputed the one over-
frugal, the other over-proud, and though both somewhat un-
sociable, yet pleasant and cordial to visitors, very hospitable
and much respected. He rode abroad in a single-seated,
single-horse chair, with a hatless, shoeless blackamoor on the
bars behind, with bare legs and feet dangling below, while
she traveled in state, in her English-built chariot and four,
with coachman and postilion and footman in bright yellow
liveries. My grandfather I never saw, but when yet an urch-
in I recall my grandmother, then very old, in a Queen Elizabeth's ruff, sitting upright and stately as a queen in her am-
ple, high-backed arm-chair, (behind which stood always her
waiting maid), an object of awe and wonder to my unaccus-
tomed eyes. They mingled little with the world, but led domestic lives; he, trimming his cedars into fanciful shapes, and
overlooking his farms, and she, holding her little state amid
her house-maidens, and superintending their work. He studied law under the distinguished Robert Carter Nicholas but
made no use of his acquisition except as a magistrate of his
county. Having mentioned Mr. Nicholas, I may not omit to
recall, to his honor, the words used by him, when, from in-
compatibility with a seat in the House of Burgesses, he resigned to that body the treasureship he had held for ten
years: "I leave the office of Treasurer," he said, "with clean
hands, certainly with empty ones,"—which his known simple
habits, and large bounty made at once famous.

I add from "Bristol Parish" (an interesting mine of old Church and family records by the Rev. Philip Slaughter), "Thomas Bolling had several children who were deaf and dumb. He sent his eldest, John, to Edinburgh in 1771, and put him under the care of Thomas Braidwood, the famous and most successful teacher of speech to deaf mutes then, or perhaps ever, known. The others, Thomas and Mary, followed in 1775, and they all remained at Braidwood's Institute during the American Revolution, returning to 'Cobb's' in 1783. John died soon after his return."

NOTICE F.

JOHN BOLLING[5] was a man of great stature, of many good qualities, but long of very dissipated habits. Devoting his time to hunting, racing, and all manner of idle amusements and indulgences, but, above all, to hard drink, he came to be called, contemptuously, "the old Indian"; for the Indians, drugged by the Circe cup of the insidious white man—as where have they not been?—were falling before its delirating effects faster than even before their arms, and now, transformed from their original nature, debauched and degraded, their very name had become in the mouths of their undoers a by-word and reproach. But for the white man there seems, happily, to be a possible stopping point in his downward career, denied to the immodifiable Indian, and this gentleman furnished an instance of it. Marrying, in middle age, a lady of great refinement and beauty (the sister of President Jefferson), her gentle ministerings and sweet influence are said to have won him away from his unworthier attachments, and now reformed, his later years, prolonged to the patriarchial term of three score and ten, appear to have been gilded once more with the respect and consideration of all around him.

NOTICE G.

ROBERT BOLLING,[5] of "Chellow," was "a lover of wisdom, and esteemed it more precious than rubies." He was educated at Wakefield, in England, by the celebrated Dr. Clarke. He was learned in many languages, and wrote the "Memoirs of the Bolling Family" in the French tongue, a translation of which, by John Robertson, was edited and printed by T. H. Wynne, Richmond, 1869. He was fond of Music and Poetry, and of the juice of the grape, but not to excess, and planted and wrote verses about, vineyards, and named a son Lenæus, after the heathen God of Wine. He was of a domestic turn and affectionate disposition, and losing early his first wife, "his soul mourned its lost companion in tones sad as the voice of the turtle bereaved of its mate." I extract from his Lament, as a specimen of his poetic faculty and loving nature, as well as because characteristic of the prevalent taste of the day, a few lines: "Alas! these lofty groves, feathered warblers, limpid rivulets, their scaly people and painted margins delight not me. With my beloved, departed are their charms; her finger showeth not their beauties; her lips of roses move no longer in their praise." He was patriotic, but unambitious, and such estimation was he held in, that the popularity which he did not seek, followed him, and though refusing to be a candidate, or engage in the canvass, or even leave his home on election day, he yet received *every vote given* in his county for the House of Burgesses, which, going in good health to attend on in Williamsburg, he sickened a few days after, and died, untimely, in the thirty-second year of his age.

NOTICE H.

ARCHIBALD BOLLING.[5]—I cite from "Opuscula," a little work of Judge John Robertson:

"He was of ordinary stature, but great round the body, and loved the ease of a private life, and esteemed book learning of little value.

"And he read no book but the Scriptures, for in them he said was eternal life, the one thing needful, and all books that taught the same were useless, and other knowledge was foolishness, and led men into error and sin.

"And he read his Bible, and had prayer for his household morning and night, and had a set of little Blackamoor singers to sing hymns with him as in the days of David, and after prayers he played on the viol.

"And when rebuked by Pharisees he reproved them in turn, telling them that King David, the man after God's own heart, and all Israel played before the Lord on all manner of instruments, and danced before Him with all their might.

"He was married four times, and told his last wife if she should die before him he would marry again, for it was God's own proverb, that it was not good man should be alone, and it was a point of conscience with him to fulfil the Scriptures.

"Like unto the old patriarch, Jacob, he was a plain man, and when first married he lived in a log cabin at Buffalo Lick, now 'Mount Athos,' in Campbell County, and afterwards in an humble dwelling in Buckingham.

"He was frugal, but hospitable and kind to all, especially to the poor, and he took no thought of filthy lucre, and despised all trade and traffic, for in his spirit was no covetousness nor guile.

"And he suffered his mighty forests to stand untouched by the axe, and his fruitful fields to grow up in briars and thorns.

"He was kindly affectioned to all men, especially to his own kin, and these he visited yearly at their distant abodes.

"All his labors were labors of love and charity, in striving to follow the example of Him who went about doing good, his only care being to lay up treasures in Heaven, and he died as he had lived, with a conscience void of offence toward God and toward man.

"And all the days of Archibald Bolling were about seventy and nine years."

NOTICE I.

ELIZABETH RANDOLPH,[5] who married RICHARD KIDDER MEADE.—Bishop Meade reports R. Kidder Meade as in the habit of saying that "General Hamilton did General Washington's head work, and he his field work." I dare say they did, but it was Washington's work they both did still. He was with Washington in all the great battles of the Revolution. To him was committed the superintendence of the execution of Major Andre, of which he always spoke with much feeling, saying he "could not forbear shedding tears at the execution of so virtuous and admirable a person, though he approved the order for it." By his first wife he had several children, but neither she nor they lived long. He married a second time Mrs. Mary, the widow of William Randolph of "Chatsworth," the mother of the distinguished Bishop Meade, whose "Old Churches, etc., of Virginia" displays the fervor alike of his piety and his patriotism, and as a mine of rare and valuable biographical and theological research, must have, for Virginians at least, an ever-increasing interest.

NOTICE J.

MARY MURRAY,[5] wife of Colonel WILLIAM DAVIES.—I am indebted to J. M. Whittle, Esq., for the following interesting contribution: "My mother, Mary Ann Davies, was a daughter of Colonel William Davies, a son of the Rev. Samuel Davies, a minister in the Presbyterian church, who resided in Hanover county, Virginia, and was a distinguished pulpit orator. Rev. Mr. Davies was a native of Delaware, and was called to Hanover when very young, where he passed all his time till called to the presidency of Princeton College, New Jersey, in 1759. He was a very active patriot in the French and Indian war in 1756, and his eloquent efforts to raise troops for the war, and encourage the fading hopes of the people, will appear from his sermons, republished in 1844, and his life by Wm. Henry Foote, D. D. His sermon, 20th July, 1755, on the defeat of Braddock, and one in August of the same year in aid of recruits in Captain Overton's company in Hanover, are the most striking. He succeeded Rev. Jonathan Edwards, the renowned religious metaphysician, in the presidency of the college, who had recently succeeded the Dr. Burr, father of Aaron Burr, so notorious. Dr. Davies died in 1761. His son, William Davies, my mother's father, was graduated at Princeton, and for some time afterwards taught in the college. Richard Stockton (signer of the Declaration of Independence), a distinguished lawyer of Princeton, became his guardian, and with him he studied the law. About the breaking out of the Revolutionary war he returned to Virginia, and settled in Blandford to practice it. His mother was a Virginia woman, a Miss Holt, and raised, I believe near or in Williamsburg. He went north with General Washington, and was engaged in some of his leading battles, and was made a Colonel. He continued in the army all the war. The particulars of his service I do not know, but he was much trusted and esteemed by General Washington, who appointed him Collector at Norfolk, in which office he remained until the election of Mr. Jefferson. In a compilation of loose and interesting historic scraps by Dr. William P. Palmer, of Richmond, lately made, will be seen a good deal of him. He is the Colonel William Davies therein mentioned. Many letters from General Washington to him, and from our most distinguished men in Virginia and elsewhere, were among his papers in my father's house, which were often mentioned within my recollection, but were destroyed in a disastrous fire in March, 1821. After the Revolution he was appointed to settle the account between Virginia and the other States, which kept him for several years at New York and Philadelphia, the first capitals after the formation of the Federal Constitution. From the library he left, and the traces through my mother's musical and other school-books of his hand-writing, as well as my knowledge of his estimation by Governor Tazewell, Judge Marshall, Major Gibbon, Colonel Gamble, Colonel Carrington, George Keith Taylor, etc., etc., his highly cultivated mind and taste are learned. He married Mary, then the young widow of Alexander Gordon, a Scotch merchant of Petersburg, Virginia, who had been Mary Murray, a daughter of James Murray and his wife Ann, who was daughter of John Bolling and Mary V. Kennon, his wife."

NOTICE K.

"ELIZABETH BOLLING,[6] wife of WILLIAM ROBERTSON.—I quote from the "Opuscula," of Judge John Robertson:

"William Robertson, who married Elizabeth Bolling, was tall, well-shaped and well-favored, of a cheerful nature but serious countenance, and much given to meditation on the wisdom and works of God.

"He had a generous, humane, and affectionate heart, and when fallen from the height of abundance into poverty, was yet ready to share with those more needy, the pittance that was left.

"The heaviest afflictions he bore with resignation and firmness, never doubting the final justice and mercy of Heaven.

"He believed the whole duty of man was that summed up by the prophet Micah—'Do justly, love mercy, and walk humbly before God.'

"On a seal of pebble, brought by him from the loved land of his fathers, transparent as glass, was engraved his family device, viz: a dove and a serpent, the symbols of innocence and wisdom, with the motto—'Virtutis Gloria Merces.'

"And this motto and the precept of the prophet were lamps unto his feet and lights unto his path.

"When no longer able to enjoy the beautiful of nature or

the pleasures of life, and weary of his long journey, he gladly received the proffered arm of man's best friend, unterrified at the thought of entering into the dark valley and the shadow that separates Time from Eternity, nay, hopefully assured of enjoying beyond it the glorious reward he had ever endeavored to deserve by exemplary virtues.

"He lived seventy-nine years, and was buried, as was his wife, afterwards, at about the same age, in the family burying-ground at 'Cobbs.'

"Alas! alas! that ancient family mansion, 'Cobbs'; that old seat of hospitality and mirth; for it hath become a ruin and a desolation."

My father was first a merchant in Petersburg, but though frugal and industrious, seems to have had no aptitude for trade, and his ventures in merchandizing and afterwards mining, all failing, he found himself, now past middle life, reduced to poverty. He then studied law and had just commenced to practice, when an offer from Richmond of an humble place in the Virginia Bank, but assuring him a living, led him to that city. He was soon advanced to be Clerk of the Council of State, and afterwards, and long, was a Member of that body. His gentle, yet firm and upright carriage in life won and kept him many good friends, among whom I may name Mr. Monroe and Governor Page.

My mother was the fitting partner of such a man, living but for him, her children, and the social circle, of which she was a cherished member.

As my father grafted a new, and not mean, stock on the Bollings, I may be pardoned for straying a little aside to make a brief allusion to it. It was that of the Robertsons of Strowan.* His relationship to them, how near or remote I do not know, he was made acquainted with by an Uncle, Arthur, then (1766) Chamberlain of the city of Glasgow, to whom he was sent from Virginia at sixteen, to attend the schools there, and with whom he spent two years. After-

---

*These Robertsons are, now, from comparatively recent discovery of old documents, believed to be lineally descended from Duncan, King of Scotland. Those who are curious to know on what grounds, I refer to Brown's "History of the Highlands" and a work not long since published by direction of Queen Victoria, called (I think) the "Clans of Scotland."

wards, also, he visited him on becoming of age. The heroic devotion to the Stuarts of the celebrated Alexander Robertson, with the splendid and varied qualities which accompanied and adorned it, "honor, heroism, humanity, poetry, learning, and wit," preserved in the "Baron of Bradwardine" of Scott's immortal romance, though they led to the forfeiture of all the territorial possessions of his family, yet secured forever the glory of his name. The great Historian and Divine, William Robertson, Lord Brougham, Patrick Henry, and Mr. Gladstone, all of the stock of Struan, also illustrate its record, and have added, by broader services to their kind and on a higher theatre, new claims on the public gratitude and estimation, to those established by their illustrious progenitor.

NOTICE L.

WILLIAM BOLLING.[6]—This gentleman inherited and settled at "Cobbs," but afterwards removed to his fine estate, on James river in Goochland county, "Bolling Hall." He was of a retiring disposition but much respected. He established, while at "Cobbs," the first institution for the education of the Deaf and Dumb seated in America, which, the prospectus states "has been established at Cobbs, near Petersburg, Virginia and is conducted by Mr. J. Braidwood, a descendant of the late Thomas and John Braidwood, of Edinburg and London." It came to an unlucky end, unfortunately, after an experiment of several years, but through no want of proficiency in the Professor. Mr. Braidwood fell into bad habits, contracted large debts with the merchants of Petersburg, and suddenly fled to the North. In 1818 he returned to Richmond, friendless, penniless, and almost naked, and applied to Colonel William Bolling for aid. Mr. Bolling associated Braidwood with the Rev. Mr. Kilpatrick, then living at Manchester, and put his son, William A. Bolling, under his care. There were six or seven pupils. Braidwood demeaned himself well for some months, but then again became so dissipated that Mr. Kilpatrick was forced to dissolve all connection with him. Braidwood finally fell to be bar-keeper in a tavern, where he died, a victim to the bottle, in 1819 or 1820. Colonel Bolling was public-spirited and patriotic, often representing his County in the Legislature, and winning his commission in the war of 1812.

NOTICE M.

THOMAS BOLLING.[6]—I cite from "Bristol Parish"—"Thomas was a miracle of accomplishments. His articulation became so good that his family and friends understood him in conversation and in reading aloud. He died in the sixty-seventh year of his age at 'Gayment' (the residence of his niece, Mrs. J. H. Bernard), in Caroline County. The late Judge Robertson (his nephew), in an obituary printed in the *Richmond Enquirer*, February 18, 1836, said of him: 'He composed and wrote in a peculiar, clear, and graphic style, and attained an artificial faculty of speech almost equal to natural. His grace of manner, vivacity and power of imitation, made him the wonder and admiration of strangers and the delight of friends and relatives.' "

NOTICE N.

LENÆUS BOLLING[6] imbibed all the spirit of William and Mary, was brave, generous, public-spirited, studious of learning, temperate, upright, cheerful, saving, but not sordid, and a lover of truth. Health was denied him for much public usefulness. A single session of the Legislature would prostrate him—to return at each decade again to be disabled. His leading maxim was Burke's, "manly, moral and regulated liberty," to which deeming restricted suffrage to be essential, he vehemently opposed the successfully projected removal of the freehold qualification of the voters, which had been handed down to us in Virginia by our fathers from 1699. He was tall, erect, swarthy, with the straight black hair and eyes of the Indian, and with strong sympathies for that decaying race.

NOTICE O.

POWHATAN BOLLING[6] was also educated at William and Mary College, but was a man rather of action than speculation, of fine physique, and of strong passions, fearless and honorable, and somewhat eccentric, both in dress and conduct. His dress was uniformly for years "a scarlet coat, white waistcoat, blue pantaloons, and a three-cornered cocked hat." It was not safe to remark on this fanciful get-up.

One of the erratic feats tradition tells of his half-tamed and insubordinate nature, is of his pursuing a wagoner who had trespassed on a forbidden road, and on his refusing to halt to shoot dead the horse under him. His gun now empty, and the wagoner clambering quickly back into his wagon for the well-understood rifle, Mr. Bolling retreated, but not quick enough, and the splendid thorough-bred he was riding received the deadly load intended for its rider. He was at some distance from his house, and the time lost in returning to it and obtaining a remount, had enabled his adversary to baffle pursuit. His hasty temper involved him in several duels. He was a skilled and ardent musician, and his violin, made in Germany in 1646, was recently and is probably still extant. He was an opponent of John Randolph for a seat in Congress, waging no mean or unequal contest even with that redoubtable champion, having been beaten by but five votes.

NOTICE P.

BLAIR BOLLING[6] would have been a hero with the opportunity. He had all the daring, devotion and fearlessness to make one. Once, about 1823 or 1824, returning with him on a coasting vessel from a visit we had made together to New York, he gave signal evidence of his courage. It had been reported at New York that a piratical vessel had been observed hovering about our coasts. As we were nearing Cape Henry a suspicious looking craft, and very erratic in her motions, was seen some miles off our starboard bow. After some quite unintelligible gyrations she bore right down on us. Our captain turned pale with fear, and the whole of the little crew was totally demoralized. This was no doubt the reported pirate. The captain, as she neared us, distinctly saw through his glass, he said, a cannon on her deck, and men crouching beside her bulwarks. One solitary rusty old musket was our whole armament. All but Bolling counselled and prepared to surrender. He loaded the musket, and despite the Captain's decision declared his purpose, if he stood alone, to kill the first man that touched our deck. The pirate luffed up quite close to us, and when we were expecting every moment a shot from her, hailed and begged us to give him his reckoning, as he had quite lost it, and did not know where he was! But Bolling had never changed color or purpose, sitting ready with his old musket at the taffrail. His after career as Captain of the "State Guard" (in his day a turbulent and refractory band) furnished many practical proofs of the dauntless spirit he then exihibted. He was a stern disciplinarian, exacting from those he commanded that strict performance of duty he imposed on himself, but just and forgiving. He was of tall stature, of fine presence, and high character.

NOTICE Q.

Dr. WILLIAM TAZEWELL.—I am indebted to one of his children for a brief notice of his father. "He was prosecuting his studies at theUniversity of Edinburgh, when he was so heavily threatened with consumption that the Faculty ordered him to the south of France. When he arrived at Paris, my father having sold his patrimony to give himself an education, had spent his last *sou* for a cup of beer and a roll. He at once applied to Chief Justice Marshall, then our Envoy there. Mr. Marshall asked him if he could speak French. He replied, 'like a native.' 'Then you will answer exactly for Secretary of the American Minister (Mr. —— ——), for he understands so little French that he has to say 'Donney moi a fork,' or 'Donney moi some beef.' So my father became the Secretary of the American Minister, and his interpreter. It was during the Directory that my father was there. He attended the Botanical Lectures of the celebrated Cuvier, which he used to deliver at the Botanical Garden, a mile from Paris.

"My grandfather, Judge John Tazewell, was of Norman descent. His ancestors were Knights in the reign of William the Conqueror. Some of his brothers were Prebends of Canterbury. He died about thirty-three years of age of consumption."

NOTICE R.

JOHN RANDOLPH.[6] He was a *Lusus Naturæ*—one of those eccentric meteors, she, at times, casts athwart the skies, to at once dazzle and perplex the beholder. He stood alone of his race and kind; alone in the blinding brightness of his intellect, and in his seeming almost total destitution of heart. It seems doubtful if he ever loved a human being with natural affection—save only his Mother, and his love for her appeared so intense as to border on the supernatural. Even she whom he sought for his Bride, at almost the supreme moment when he was to bind her to his side forever, fled terrified from his embrace. On the instant, he angrily mounted his horse and never saw her again. The cause of their falling out, though dimly surmised in men's thoughts and whisperings, yet never disclosed, lies buried with them.

His delight, more particularly, perhaps, from that notable hour, appears to have been to annoy and disconcert even his satellites and friends by his arrogance and contumely, and crush his enemies under his bitter scorn—indeed all whom he touched in his orbit: friend or foe, good or bad, weak or strong, alike—and to witness their writhings or discomfiture. Let one illustration suffice. His truest friend, and one of the highest of men (Judge William Leigh), sat with him at his fireside conversing, when Mr. Randolph allowed himself to offensively contradict him. Though late in the night, Judge Leigh—Mr. Randolph making no apology—requested him to order his horse, as he would not sleep under the roof of a man who had insulted him. Mr. Randolph rose and went out apparently to fulfil his request. Instead, "the horse had escaped from the stable" (having been turned out by his order), Judge Leigh had no alternative but stay. Mr. Randolph the next morning lavished every attention on him, but offered no other atonement. Thus he dealt with his best and most prized friend. He was the impersonation of opposition and aggressiveness, though when he chose, which was rarely, nothing could exceed the elegance, refinement and charm of his manners. He stood by what *is*, hating innovation, because what *is* stands always in opposition to change and progress. He spared none, except such as he must needs have, at times, to help his ends, or minister to his ease, and these felt well paid for their complaisance by the regal smile which saved them from his spleen. With rare exceptions he sought to pull everybody down who stood in his way or opposed his views. Avarice alone (never more painfully displayed than in connection with the Russian Mission), divided with hate and scorn for his kind, the sombre empire of his bosom. He lay usually in his lonely lair, avoiding and avoided by men, and was hardly less alone in crowds than in his hermitage at Roanoke; but he let Ambition and the love of power and money prevail over his misanthropy so far as needful to secure the gratification of these engrossing aims. The victims of his eccentricities were innumerable, but none of them so wretched as himself, or so deserving to be pitied. Doubtless some secret grief, or eating worm, seamed the smooth face of his boyhood, untimely, with wrinkles and destroyed its purple bloom, preyed on the gentler traits of his original nature and left his worser powers unbalanced (at times there is good reason to believe indeed, wholly unhinged) to enjoy their carnival; the very withering or want of those moral elements, imparting an unnatural splendor and power to his intellect, and adding Titanic force to his thence unchecked sinister impulses. I am reminded, while I write, of a deer I once had. Of rare beauty, at once, and strength, he ruled imperiously over his subjects. He grew ill, became morose and dangerous, and more and more an object of terror and awe to all he approached. The herd quickly fell off to right and left as he took his way through them, and every one kept clear of him. At length, the hand that reared him was the only one whose caresses he would permit. A hidden disease was telling on him, and one of his antlers fell from his head. I missed him for a day or two, then went to seek him. At the bottom of a basin-like depression of the park, I found him, terribly emaciated, with head reverted, licking his flank. He had licked the hair off clean from a space the size of a man's hand, and still seemed trying to reach the source of his agony—and so died. I think I see in this case the explanation and atoning plea for the strange and almost unnatural fierceness that came over Mr. Randolph's spirit. Let blame fall lightly, then, on the one whom nature or fate thus dealt with in so hard a measure. His proper wretchedness might soften even his worst foe or his sorest victim, as far exceeding any that he inflicted. Let the bolt which human censure, ignorant of cause, and hence unfit to wield, might be tempted to hurl at him, be caught, timely, by that pity we all need, and leave him to be judged, where alone causes and consequences can be seen together, an unerring justice meted out. His oratory was unique, and well nigh irresistible.

I was present in 1829, when he delivered almost the last words, I believe, he ever spoke in a public capacity. He rose slowly and stood, tall, graceful and composed, before his peers—a brilliant assemblage, the Virginia Convention, of

'29, over which Madison and Marshall, surrounded by many lesser but shining lights, yet shed their setting glories. The question was on a clause providing for future amendments to the Constitution. He spoke more as an Augur, declaring the evils to come out of the provision he was examining, than as a Statesman discussing them. He used little action, as though stirred rather than contorted, by the "present Diety." His voice was clear, far-reaching through the hall—not sweet, but with something that took captive every ear, like a trumpet heard afar off at night. His eyes glitttered with their wonted brightness, nor did his fateful fore-finger forget that day its office. He denounced the clause he was assailing as carrying a condemnation with it of the instrument that contained it as a death-warrant on its brow, and covered it, and withered it, with his burning scorn. The Assembly yielded, as under the spell of a magician, a compliance that cost much trouble to the people when twenty years afterwards they wished to amend the instrument, and which a wiser firmness would have saved them from.

Mr. Randolph filled a large space in his country's eye from the dawn of his manhood to his most sorrowful death; but though always felt in her councils, he never swayed them. His life was one of wasted opportunities, and resultless energies.

No monument remains of good effected by him for his kind. Where, in a conspicuous instance—the emancipation of his slaves—he may be believed to have sought to raise one, he but aggravated the suffering he intended to relieve. He dazzled, but did not warm, and no fruits ripened in his rays. He passed—drawing our gaze of wonder as he went, but leaving only a troubled memory when he vanished.

RESUMÉ.

In surveying the above two parent, and largely determining, as well as more easily estimated, Groups—the Fifth and Sixth from the savage form of life—we may fitly pause a moment to denote generally their leading characteristics as derived through tradition, and all that is known of them. In disposition, they seem to have been mild, but firm; brave, but not aggressive; unambitious, but public spirited; affectionate with one another, and just to all. In habits, fond of pleasures, but rarely given to excess, and more commonly inclined to social and literary pursuits than hard work and enterprise, and hence constantly decaying in fortune. In talents, usually respectable, and sometimes superior, rarely deficient. In character, upright and unreproached. They formed in general that intelligent and virtuous Middle Class which everywhere forms the main pillar and stay of society and government. The Murrays, the Bollings, the Gays, the Eldridges, and their descendants, may more abundantly support this statement, though hardly more strikingly than other branches of the stock.

Burk, the Historian of Virginia (cited by Bishop Meade), writing, in 1804, of what he calls "this remnant of the imperial family of Virginia, which long ran in a single person, now increased and branched out into a numerous progeny," says: "The virtues of mildness and humanity, so eminently distinguished in Pocahontas, remain in the nature of an inheritance to her posterity. There is scarcely a scion from this stock which has not been in the highest degree amiable and respectable," and adds that he is "acquainted with several members of this family who are intelligent, and even eloquent, and if fortune keep pace with their merits, should not despair of attaining a conspicuous and even exalted station in the Commonwealth." In the after career of several of those he alluded to, most conspicuously in John Randolph, this prediction was fully verified.

NOTICE S.

THE WHITTLES.—The American head of this family, Fortescue, came to Virginia about 1799 or 1800, a young man, who had been engaged in the Irish troubles in which Robert Emmett was beheaded, and which banished Thomas Addis Emmett and other eminent men to this country. Mr. Whittle was a Protestant. He settled in Norfolk and went into business with an elder brother there, Conway, who had emigrated to Virginia soon after the Peace of 1783. His son, William Conway, entered the United States Navy and remained in it till the Secession War, when he resigned and was made a Commodore in the Confederate service. He was engaged in the naval part of the Mexican war (in which he was wounded), and in the Confederate service rendered much desultory service on York river, along the Mississippi and its tributaries and commanded the naval forces at New Orleans when it fell.

Other members of this family have won and still live to enjoy merited distinction. The author of the foregoing note stands second to no one at the Virginia bar. Stephen Decatur was Secretary of the State Convention of 1850, and William Conway, Jr., Confederates States Navy, while yet a youth, shared all the dangers and all the honors of the cruise of the Shenandoah.

RT. REV. F. M. WHITTLE, D. D., LL D.

Of the immediate subject of this notice I am indebted to the Rev. John J. Lloyd, St. Thomas' Church, Abingdon, for the following sketch:

Rt. Rev. Francis McNeece Whittle, D. D., LL.D., fifth Bishop of the Diocese of Virginia, was born in Mecklenburg county, Virginia, July 7th, 1823.

His father, Fortescue Whittle, Esq., of County Antrim, Ireland, settled in Norfolk, Va., early in present century.

His mother was Mary Davies, grand-daughter of Rev. Samuel Davies, President of Princeton College, and daughter of Colonel William Davies of the Revolutionary army, aid to General Washington, and appointed by him collector of Norfolk, Va.

Mrs. Whittle's mother was Mary Murray, of Chesterfield county.

Bishop Whittle graduated at the Theological Seminary of Virginia in the summer of 1847; was ordered Deacon in St. Paul's Church, Alexandria, Va., July 16, the same year, and was ordained Priest in St. John's, Charleston, Va. (now West Virginia), October 8th, 1848, by Bishop William Meade. He was successively Rector of Kanawha Parish, Kanawha county, Virginia (1847-'49); St. James'-Northam Parish, Goochland county, Virginia (1849-'52); Grace, Berryville, Va. (1852-'57); St. Paul's Louisville, Kentucky (1857-'68).

At the Council of the Diocese of Virginia, held 1867, he was elected Assistant Bishop of Virginia, and was consecrated in St. Paul's, Alexandria, April 30, 1868, by Bishops Johns of Virginia, Lee of Delaware, and Bedell of Ohio.

He received the degree of D. D. from the Theological Seminary of Ohio, 1867, and that of LL.D. from the College of William and Mary.

He became Bishop April 5, 1876. In 1877 the Diocese was divided, the State, known as West Virginia, being erected into a separate Diocese.

He married, May 15, 1848, Emily Cary, daughter of Wilson Miles Cary Fairfax, and Lucy A. Griffith, his wife, and who was great-grand-daughter of Rev. Bryan, Lord Fairfax, Rector of Falls Church Parish, Virginia, and of Rev. David Griffith, D. D., Chaplain and Surgeon in the Army of the Revolution, and the first Bishop elect of Virginia.

NOTICE T.

THOMAS BOLLING ROBERTSON[7] was educated at William and Mary, and commenced the practice of law at Petersburg. There he was intimate with John Thomson, who, as "Curtius," disputing, *passibus equis*, with John Marshall, already renowned, achieved, at twenty-four, a celebrity that no one before or since in Virginia so early attained. For his death, immediately ensuing, he expressed his grief in very touching verses. There, too, he became acquainted with Burk, the Historian, who was much attached to him, and who, dying soon after, bequeathed his only son, Junius, afterwards a Judge in Louisiana ('twas all he left besides his book) to his care.

In 1807, he received from Mr. Jefferson the appointment of Secretary to the new Territory of Louisiana from which time he resided in that State. He was the first Representative of the State in the Congress of the United States, and served with distinction and acceptability to his constituents in that body for several sessions, then retiring from impaired health and increasing distaste for Congressional life. He was an efficient supporter of the administration of Mr. Madison, who divided with Mr. Lowndes (his ideal statesman) his highest admiration and confidence. Late in life, he said that of all the public men he had known, these two he considered the purest and most disinterested. Mr. Clay he ranked for his ambition only a step below them. While in Congress, Mr. Randolph (John) made some offensive reflection on a vote he had given in favor of a duty on sugar (his general views being anti-tariff), and refusing to apolgize, my brother challenged him. The challenge declined on the ground, as assigned by himself, that he did not hold himself bound to meet such demands whensoever any gentleman chose to feel himself aggrieved. My brother soon afterwards paid a short visit to Paris. As a member of the American Congress, at that period but rare visitants to Europe, he was treated with much consideration. He was present in the Hall of the Deputies at the sitting at which Bonaparte, calm, and apparently confident in the invincibility of his Eagles, took leave of the Deputies on his fateful departure for Waterloo. He remained in Paris during the Hundred Days, saw rolled into the city the captured cannon, announcing a great victory for the French, followed instantly after by Bonaparte in person, flying from his mighty disaster; and again saw him, now when he came before the same Body in his despair to abdicate Empire, and, as it proved, even personal liberty forever, as calm and as self collected as, when going, he left them in the flush of his hopes. A graphic account of the "Events in Paris" was given by Mr. Robertson in letters to his family, written while they were transpiring, which were published first in the *Richmond Enquirer,* and afterwards by Carey, of Philadelphia, in book form and went through several editions. His Congressional career ended, he was soon after elected Governor of Louisiana. Serving his constitutional term, he resumed the practice of law in New Orleans, and was soon made Attorney-General, and shortly after appointed United States District Judge for Louisiana. His health now greatly broken (*dulcis reminiscitur Argos*), he came to Virginia in the hope of restoring it amid the scenes and friends of his youth, and in the society of his aged parents (from all which neither time nor distance had ever for a moment estranged his affections), but died as he had lived, honorably poor, at the White Sulphur Springs, where the tomb erected over him by his widow still marks his last resting place. He was a man of extensive information and enlarged views, of clear mind, of elevated aims, of simple tastes, a lover of flowers and plants and versed in their lore, of spotless integrity, of warm affections, and of immovable firmness; but a gentle nature was so blended in him, with decision of character mirrored in a face of rare beauty, that he was as generally beloved, as he was universally respected. Among those who honored him with their warm friendship, and possessed his, were Mr. Lowndes, Mr. Clay, General Zachary Taylor and Lieutenant-General Scott—a friendship which, could they speak, none would be so ready as themselves to acknowledge, was as honoring to them as to him. When years after his death the writer was casually introduced to General, then President Taylor, the latter observing some likeness, and inquiring the relationship, embraced him as a brother, and opened himself to him on the delicate topics that then engaged him as he might have done to a tried friend. Such friendships, more than office, eulogies, or monuments, best attest worth.

NOTICE U.

JOHN ROBERTSON.[7]—The subject of this notice was for many years of his life in the service of the State, either as a member of the House of Representatives of the United States, or as Circuit Judge or as Attorney-General of the State. In all these public capacities his many good qualities, his boldness, his frankness, his generosity, and his high sense of honor, together with his ingenuity and ability of intellect, earned him the respect and affection of all who knew him well. His mind was marked both by ingenuity and ability, and following its operations fully and fearlessly, as he was wont to do, he was sometimes led to conclusions which were regarded as extreme, as he was apt to express them without fear upon any singularity of opinion, or from any deviation of common sentiment. Of this last he was less in awe than any public man of my acquaintance. He thought freely, spoke boldly, and suffered neither fear, favor nor affection to seduce him from what he believed to be truth. Had truth indeed been lying at the bottom of a deep well, he is one of the few I have known who I believe to be capable of jumping after it to preserve and display it. In doing this, he cared for no prejudices which he might provoke, and shrunk from no denunciations he might stir up, but fearlessly followed the germs he was pursuing, without regard for the difficulties into which it might lead him.

The friend who has written these few lines did not concur with Judge Robertson in all his opinions, but he never failed to admire the spirit in which they were conceived and expressed. If any man in his course through life has earned for himself the epigraph of "honest and true" on his memorial slab, surely that man was Judge John Robertson.

R. M. T. HUNTER.

To the foregoing tribute of its eminent author, who knew the subject of it almost alone by political association, I add a few other traits and incidents of Judge Robertson's character and career.

He was born at "Belfield," his father's residence, below Petersburg, and came with the family to Richmond about 1803. There he spent his life, except his college years at Williamsburg, and his closing ones at his country home, "Mount Athos," near Lynchburg. Adopting the profession of Law he soon won distinction, and was made Attorney-General of the State in 188–. He was learned, laborious, and conscientious in the discharge of every duty. No wealth, position, or influence, could qualify his zeal or daunt his efforts, or baffle them when exerted in the cause of right. When engaged in such a cause, whether as Advocate or Judge, none felt solicitude about the result, for all knew there was no art nor ability could deceive his vigilance, or corrupt his fidelity, or bias or betray his judgment, or elude his pursuit.

In politics he was a *doctrinal* Democrat of the Jefferson school, but never a thrall to a party. He was a ready, stinging, and aggressive debater. In his canvass for Congress, his arraignment of Jackson was so sharp that the latter's admirers sought to silence him by persistent shouts of "Hurrah for Jackson!" "I beg pardon, my friends," said he, in the first lull of the clamor, "for having said there was no argument in defence of Jackson's conduct I could not answer. There is one—it is 'Hurrah for Jackson!'" He was little troubled afterwards by interruptions, and carried his election. In Congress his abilities were highly estimated. By his friends he was called a stickler for the Constitution, so strict was his loyalty to it; and an illustrative story was invented on him by his witty and waggish friend, Waddy Thompson, of South Carolina, that once being in Washington, and supposed about to die, he begged him as his last request not to allow him to be buried at public expense, for he thought it would be clearly unconstitutional.

In our late civil embroilment, though not one more sternly than he demanded immunity for his State from interference with her domestic system, yet was he known to so earnestly deprecate violent measures, as long as honorably avoidable, that he was sent by Virginia to her sister States of the South to urge forbearance, while ex-President Tyler was dispatched on a similar mission to President Buchanan. Failing of success, they both dedicated their closing years to the defence, in the high posts assigned them, of the invaded rights and territory of their State and the South. Among other evidences of his devotion may be mentioned his giving his town residence to the Cause as a soldier's hospital.

His mind was always aglow with activity, seeking recreation from severer labors only in roaming over, and lovingly cultivating, the fields of Literature. While those labors denied him its heaviest harvests, yet his tragedy of "Riego, the Spanish Martyr," his principal oblation at the shrine of letters; his "Opuscula" teeming with the finest specimens of satire as of praise, and of felicitous portraiture; his Scholarly address at the opening of the Anthenaeum at Richmond, etc., evidence by their breadth of thought, richness of imagery and beauty of diction, that, in spite of the drawbacks alluded to, he attained a very high order of literary achievement. I cite a few lines of his "Riego," which, though I know that such mere shreds can do no justice to the work, may yet serve to show that my praise of it is not wholly undeserved.

Riego speaks to Diaz, a youth, of General Washington:

> "Why name that name
> Unknown to Heraldry, though brighter ne'er
> Was blazoned on the Rolls of Fame—which echoes
> In terror from the Palace dome, but carries
> Joy to the Cotter's roof! His brow severe,
> Of native dignity, no jeweled crown
> E'er tarnished, but, instead, the civic oak,
> Mingled with laurel boughs, his temples bound.
> As by one soul inspired, the undaunted Gaul
> And spotless Chief breasted the storm, nor ceased
> Their toils till they had won a nation's Liberty;
> The world's esteem, the approving smile of Heaven.
> Freedom's unsceptred son, his Country's Saviour,
> Now dwells in bliss; his glory freshening in
> The stream of Time, and still while that stream flows,
> Shall his loved memory be hymned in praise."

His own private traits were such as to attach, by their sympathetic tenderness, those he loved and valued to him with hooks of steel, but he looked severely on the bad, the hypocritical and the proud, and was not beloved by such. Nothing so awoke him to effort as oppression and fraud, and while knave and spoiler shrank from the swoop of his talons, the widow and the orphan nestled in safety under his protecting wing. Shortly before his death, when past four score, he wrote of himself this

"PRE-OBITUARY."

"When my long pilgrimage is over, I desire no invited company nor services beyond those of laying me in my last bed. Let those who may happen to be present—my household friends, kind neighbors and faithful servants—perform for me that service; nor let them sorrow over me, who has had his share of the blessings as well as the sufferings no mortal can escape, and who, though repenting the many aberrations of a frail nature, has never felt the pangs of a guilty conscience, and is not left as one without hope."

NOTICE V.

WYNDHAM ROBERTSON.[7] Save as the compiler of this little work, rendering it perhaps a duty to his readers, this Notice would have been spared. I will limit it mainly to points that more or less tend to inspire confidence in the trustworthiness, or, at least, good faith of my compilation. I finished an imperfect education (but the best always which the *res angusta* of my parents, pinching even their own frugal housekeeping for the purpose, would admit of) by two interrupted sessions at William and Mary under the brilliant presidency of Dr. John Augustine Smith. That gentleman's flashing and suggestive lectures waked to new life the dormant faculties of his pupils, and taught to them, too, the independent and fearless use of them, which he practiced himself. It was a lesson which, aglow with the fresh excitement, his classes were swift to apply, in clamorous disputation, as soon as they issued from the lecture room.

I was admitted to the bar in 1824. In 1827 I made a short visit to London and Paris. In 1830 I was made Councillor of State. One the occasion of the French Revolution, in the same year, I was called on to give utterance to the enthusiasm of the city of Richmond by a public address at the capitol. Processions and parades, flags, banners, bands of music and cannon, further testified to the warm sympathy of the outpoured crowds of its citizens. Sharing the fervor of the hour, I was fortunate in interpreting the general feeling and in winning that favor and confidence of the City, which, often experienced, was never withdrawn during my long residence in it—always a source to me of, I hope a legitimate, pride, and which I trust I shall be pardoned for alluding to.

In 1833 I was again elected to the Council of the State, now reduced from eight to three members.

In 1834, at the first meeting of the James River and Kanawha Company, I proposed, in lieu of the projected canal, a measure that looked to a railroad connection in lieu of by canal between Richmond and the Great West. Although, from the fear of hazarding a crude and unproven system against a sure and tried one, it was decisively defeated, it had the distinguished sanction of such men as Dr. Brockenbrough, Judge Nicholas, Moncure Robinson and Judge Robertson. The supreme commercial advantages to Richmond and Virginia that would have been secured to them by opening her Western Railroad connections in advance of all others, and which other States hastened to appropriate, need not be dwelt on.

On the 31st of March, 1836, becoming Lieutenant-Governor, Governor Tazewell resigned his office on the same day into my hands for the remaining year of his term. It was unmarked except by the rapid spread of abolitionism, to which I called the attention of the Legislature, and recommended that Commissioners should be sent to the Northern States, appealing to them to unite in measures to arrest, and, if possible, compose, the threatened troubles. But the recommendation was not acted on.

The Legislature elect being largely Democratic, the Whigs declined contesting the Executive Offices in 1837-38. Immediately after I was elected to the Legislature from the city of Richmond, and was continued in it, until I removed to the country in 1841. Returning to Richmond in 1858, in the midst of the troubles that soon resulted in our late war, my old constituents again demanded my services, and continued to require them to the close of the contest. A friend to peace and the Union, I actively opposed the overtures of South Carolina in 1859 for a Southern Convention, as, in my opinion, calculated only to still more imperil them. After that State and others had seceded, I still urged a refusal on the part of Virginia to follow them, and reported (as the organ of a committee), the day it met, 7th January, 1861, the resolution known as the Anti-Coercion Resolution, in effect rejecting secession, but declaring if coercion were employed by the Federal Government against the seceded States, Virginia would fight with the South. The resolution was adopted with much unanimity, and the State now addressed itself to measures of reconcilement, all of which I advocated, and some proposed. All failed, and soon Mr. Lincoln's Proclamation of war, presenting the contingency she had provided for, Virginia stood upon her defence. In this, and all after measures in aid of the war, I fully concurred. And now, after twenty years' experience of yet unripened results, I have no regrets, nor repent a single act of my State, or myself, in these unhappy affairs—welcoming the end of slavery, but still believing it would have been reached without the horrors of war.

In 1863 a Bill "to fix prices of food," &c., was proposed, which believing to be fraught with the direst mischief, I earnestly opposed and contributed to defeat.

In 1864 some hundreds of my constituents assembled and passed a resolution demanding of their representatives to support a similar bill or resign. I had no difficulty in refusing to a committee their peremptory demand of a compliance with their resolutions, but finding afterwards that all my colleagues had yielded to it, and left apparently in the position of misrepresenting my constituents, and stripped of influence, I resigned in a note to the House, and at once left my seat. Immediately after, that body did me the honor unanimously to request the withdrawal of my resignation till the wishes of my constituents could be better ascertained, and sent a committee to me to convey their wishes. I, of course, acceded to the request. A formal poll was held in the city by order of the Council, and my views sustained by my constituents, as afterwards by the House.

Since the close of the war, bowing to the arbitrament of the sword as final between the States, and deprecating the restoration of slavery, now abolished, as earnestly as I had opposed the abolition of it, I have been wholly withdrawn from active politics, except indeed in heartily co-operating in every proposed measure for healing and reconcilement between the States, and for the redintegration of Virginia, and have found gratifying occupation in part in preparing this compilation, and also a "Vindication of the course of Virginia throughout the Slave Controveresy," probably soon to be published.

NOTICE W.

CHARLES JOSEPH CABELL, born 1789. He graduated at William and Mary. Read law under Governor William H. Cabell and William Wirt. Mr. Wirt pronounced him the greatest man of his age in Virginia. He emigrated to New Orleans, and in a few months took rank with Philip R. Grymes, —— Holmes, and Edward Livingston—so said *Governor Thomas Bolling Robertson.* He was three times called to the field (so called) of honor: First, with General Ben. Jones, then of Amelia, afterwards of Alabama; second, with Dr. Upshaw, at New Orleans, but who went from King and Queen, Va.; third, with a Mr. Nicholson, of New Orleans, a nephew of Lawyer Abner L. Duncan, who instigated the deed. He died of yellow fever on the 23d of November, 1810, in the city of New Orleans, aged only twenty-one years.—*From Notes of the late General Ben W. S. Cabell.*

RESUME.

THE POCAHONTAS STOCK.—In view of all I have heard, read or known of them, I think it may be fairly said that they were more prudent than enterprising, more wasteful than liberal, more amiable then censorious, more respected than distinguished, more honest than able, more patriotic than indifferent, more conservative than radical, more pious than bigoted, and while a few fell to the depths of worthlessness, but none to crime, a few also rose to the height of genius and virtue.

ADDENDUM.

Of JENNY ELDRIDGE,[5] known to my boyhood by everybody as "Old Cousin Jenny," and to whose active inquisitions owes much, I am enabled by a recent communication to say that she was a family celebrity, disinguished for her alertness of body and mind—a bright wit, a fine memory, and especially for devotion to her Indian blood, and all its lore and tradition. It was said of her that she could call the name and kinship of every descendant of Pocahontas. She was the chief storehouse, therefore, and authority of her day of everything known concerning her family in the minutest particulars before and during her time. To her is due the preserved knowledge of the headspring of many of its branches, which else had been irrecoverably lost.